# UNDERNEATH THE SYNTAX

## A Primer on Programming Fundamentals

EDISON MOOERS

Gibidda Press

First edition, 2026

Published by Gibidda Press
Germantown, Maryland
gibidda.com

ISBN 979-8-9972857-0-8

*For anyone who has ever tried to learn something on their own and felt overwhelmed, and for the people who took the time to help me understand.*

# Contents

# Introduction: Why This Book Exists

## Where This Started for Me

I'm self-taught. It started with a hand-me-down: an uncle of mine worked for IBM, and passed along an old Tandy TRS-80 he no longer needed. It had no hard drive. It didn't even have a disk drive of any kind. What it had was a manual, and a proprietary dialect of BASIC built directly into the machine.

So I sat down with that manual, and I taught myself, one concept at a time. There was no course, no curriculum, no one to ask when something didn't make sense. Just the manual, the machine, and enough curiosity to keep turning the page. I ate it up. Everything I've built since, every language I've picked up, every system I've designed, grew out of that one hand-me-down computer and a manual I worked through cover to cover.

## Starting Slow, and Why That Mattered

Here's the part of that story that matters most for this book. That TRS-80 forced me to start slow, because there was nothing else on offer. No frameworks. No libraries. No package manager offering a thousand shortcuts before I understood what any of them were shortcuts for. Just variables, loops, and conditionals, introduced one at a time, in a manual that assumed I knew absolutely nothing and built up from there.

I remember exactly what it felt like to learn each fundamental as its own, complete idea, and then to genuinely feel the ground get more solid underneath me as each new piece stacked on top of the last one. By the time I moved on to more capable machines and more capable languages, I wasn't learning programming from scratch anymore. I was just learning new vocabulary for ideas I already had a firm grip on.

## A Career Built on That Same Foundation

My professional path into programming started with COBOL, writing and maintaining commercial accounting software, and later doing Y2K remediation on systems that, even then, were already old. From there, I moved through C#, .NET, SQL Server, and enterprise architecture, across healthcare, legal, financial services, and technology, building things throughout the late 1990s and 2000s while completing both a Bachelor's and a Master's degree in Information Technology, and earning a Microsoft Certified Application Developer certification, at night, while working full-time. Somewhere in there, I designed a security architecture for handling payment data that went on to influence how tokenization is still approached in that industry today.

None of that came from a single, tidy educational path. It came from the same thing that manual taught me on that old Tandy: stay curious, learn one solid piece at a time, and build the next thing on top of ground that's actually solid. I've been writing software, in one form or another, for over three decades now, and I've never once stopped picking up something new.

## Why I Wrote This Book

Somewhere along the way, I noticed that learning to program today looks very different than it did when I started, and not entirely for the better. A newcomer today doesn't get handed a manual and a machine with nowhere else to look. They get handed frameworks, build tools, package managers, and an overwhelming buffet of languages, often all at once, long before anyone gives them a real, solid answer to a much simpler question: what is actually happening when this code runs?

That's the exact thing my old TRS-80 never let me skip past, simply because it had nothing else to offer. Modern languages are extraordinarily capable, but that same breadth means a beginner today rarely gets the experience I had: starting slow, sitting with one idea until it's genuinely solid, and only then building the next one on top of it. The overwhelm so many new programmers feel today isn't a sign that they're not cut out for this. It's a sign that they've been handed the whole toolbox before anyone showed them what any single tool is actually for.

This book is my attempt to hand someone that same slow, solid start directly, without the overwhelm, and without pretending any single language is the "right" one to begin with. Build a firm grasp of what's in these pages, and you won't just be learning to write code in one particular language. You'll be learning to think like a programmer, the way I first learned it, one fundamental at a time, in a way that travels with you into whatever language, or whatever decade, comes next.

## How to Read This Book

Part I covers the basics: what a program actually is, and the tools every single program is built from. Part II goes a level deeper, into how those fundamentals actually work underneath the surface, and introduces a handful of more advanced ideas that build directly on Part I. Part III brings it all together, with a complete working example and a tour of real, working languages, so you can see exactly where everything in this book actually shows up in practice.

This book isn't tied to one programming language, and it isn't a substitute for a language-specific tutorial. Its purpose is to give you the conceptual foundation that makes those tutorials easier to understand once you sit down with one. The examples throughout use simplified, language-neutral pseudocode so you can focus on what a program is doing before worrying about the exact punctuation any one language requires.

Not every reader here is on the way to writing a first program. Testers reasoning about how software should behave, and anyone directing an AI tool to write code and needing to judge whether the result is right, depend on this same foundation, even if they never write the punctuation themselves. If that's you, everything here still applies. You're reading for the same understanding, just putting it to a different use.

Take your time with it. There's no overwhelm here, only the fundamentals, one at a time, in the order they're meant to be learned.

# Part I: The Basics

# Chapter 1: A Brief History of Programming

## Before There Were Languages

The first computers didn't have programming languages at all. They had wires, switches, and plugboards. Programming the ENIAC in the 1940s meant physically rewiring the machine for each new task, a process that could take days. There was no "code" in the sense we mean today. There was only configuration.

The next step was machine code: raw sequences of 1s and 0s that the processor could execute directly. Every instruction, every memory address, every operation had to be written as binary. It worked, but it was slow to write and nearly impossible to read back later. A single misplaced digit could send a program somewhere it was never meant to go.

## Assembly and the First Abstraction

Assembly language was the first real abstraction layer. Instead of writing raw binary, programmers could write short mnemonic instructions, things like MOV, ADD, or JMP, and a translator program called an assembler would convert them into machine code. This was the first time a piece of software stood between the programmer and the hardware.

Assembly was still tied closely to the specific machine it ran on. Code written for one computer's processor generally wouldn't run on another. But it introduced an idea that would define the next seventy years of computing: that programmers could write in something more human, and let a tool handle the translation into something a machine could run.

## Punch Cards and Early Batch Processing

For much of the mid-20th century, programs were entered on punch cards, stiff paper cards with holes representing data and instructions. A program might be a physical stack of hundreds of cards, fed into a card reader in a specific order. Drop the stack, and you had a serious problem.

This was the era of batch processing. You didn't sit at a terminal and get instant feedback. You submitted your stack of cards, waited, sometimes for hours or overnight, and came back to see whether your program had run correctly or crashed on line one. Debugging was slow, expensive, and often not interactive at all.

## High-Level Languages Arrive

The 1950s and 60s brought the first high-level languages, ones designed to be readable by people, not just translatable to machine instructions.

FORTRAN (1957) was built for scientific and mathematical computing, and is still in use in some scientific computing contexts today.

COBOL (1959) was designed for business data processing, with a deliberately English-like syntax so that non-programmers could, in theory, read it.

LISP (1958) introduced ideas, like treating code as data, that still influence functional programming today.

These languages needed compilers: programs that translated the high-level source code into machine code the processor could actually run. The compiler became the new go-between, and it meant a single program could, with adjustments, run on more than one type of machine.

## Structured Programming

By the late 1960s and into the 1970s, a problem was becoming obvious: as programs grew larger, they were turning into tangled messes. Code jumped from place to place unpredictably (often using a GOTO statement), and it became genuinely difficult to reason about what a program would do.

Structured programming emerged as a response. The core idea was that programs should be built from a small set of predictable control structures: sequences, conditionals (if/else), and loops, rather than arbitrary jumps. Languages like C (1972) embraced this philosophy and became foundational, influencing the syntax of countless languages that followed.

This era is also when many of the "fundamentals" this book covers, variables, conditionals, loops, functions, became broadly standardized in the way we still recognize them today.

## Object-Oriented Programming

Through the 1980s and 90s, a different way of organizing code gained popularity: object-oriented programming, or OOP. Instead of thinking of a program purely as a sequence of steps, OOP encouraged thinking in terms of objects, bundles of data and the behavior that acts on that data.

Languages like Smalltalk pioneered these ideas, and C++ brought them to a much wider audience by building object-oriented features on top of C. Java (1996, the year of its first official public release, though an early alpha had circulated the year before) pushed OOP further into the mainstream, with a strong emphasis on portability across different machines. This is also the era covered in this book's chapter on objects, classes, and structures.

## The Modern, Multi-Paradigm Era

Since the 2000s, most widely used languages have stopped fitting neatly into a single paradigm. Modern languages tend to borrow freely: object-oriented features, functional programming ideas, dynamic typing, and static typing all show up side by side, often in the same language.

Python (first released 1991, but exploding in popularity from the 2000s onward) prioritized readability and simplicity.

JavaScript (1995) became the language of the web, running in every browser.

C#, Go, Rust, and Swift each emerged to solve more specific modern problems: enterprise development, simplicity at scale, memory safety without a garbage collector, and modern app development, respectively.

What's notable is that despite decades of change in syntax, tooling, and philosophy, the underlying fundamentals, variables, types, conditionals, loops, functions, have remained remarkably stable. A programmer who deeply understands those fundamentals can move between languages far more easily than one who has only memorized a single language's syntax.

That stability is the whole premise of this book.

## Looking Ahead

The rest of this book sets aside language-specific syntax entirely and focuses on the ideas that have survived every one of these eras: what a program is, how data is represented, how logic branches and repeats, and how code gets organized. Once those fundamentals are solid, learning any specific language becomes a matter of vocabulary, not a fight against overwhelm.

# Chapter 2: What a Program Actually Is

## Instructions, Not Magic

Strip away the syntax, the frameworks, and the jargon, and a program is a surprisingly simple thing: a list of instructions, carried out one after another, in order. That's it. Everything else in this book, every fundamental concept, is really just a variation on that one idea.

This matters because it's easy, especially early on, to treat a computer like it understands intent. It doesn't. A computer does not know what you're trying to accomplish. It only knows how to execute the exact instruction in front of it, then move to the next one.

## The Computer as a Very Literal-Minded Assistant

A useful way to think about a computer is as an assistant with three defining traits:

- It is extremely fast.
- It never gets tired or bored.
- It is completely, sometimes maddeningly, literal.

If you tell this assistant "make me a sandwich," it won't do anything, because that's not an instruction it knows how to carry out. But if you say "pick up the bread, place one slice on the counter, open the jar, spread its contents on the bread," it will do exactly that, and nothing more. If you forget to tell it to stop spreading when the knife reaches the edge of the bread, it may try to keep going.

This is the essence of programming: breaking a task down into a sequence of steps precise enough that a literal-minded assistant can carry them out without needing to guess what you meant.

## Execution Order

By default, a computer executes instructions in the order they appear, from top to bottom, one at a time. This is called sequential execution, and it's the default behavior of nearly every program in nearly every language.

```
step 1
step 2
step 3
```

Each step finishes completely before the next one begins. There's no getting ahead, no skipping around, unless the program is explicitly told to do so.

That "unless" is important, because later chapters are all about giving the program permission to deviate from strict top-to-bottom order:

Conditional logic lets the program skip some steps entirely, depending on a condition.

Loops let the program repeat a set of steps multiple times.

Functions let the program jump to a separate block of instructions and then return to where it left off.

Every one of these is still, underneath, just a different way of controlling which instruction gets executed next. There's no hidden mechanism beyond that.

## A Program Is a Recipe

A helpful comparison: a computer program is a lot like a recipe.

A recipe lists ingredients (data) and a sequence of steps (instructions) to transform those ingredients into a finished dish (output). It assumes nothing about what you already know beyond the literal steps written down. "Preheat the oven to 350°F" isn't a suggestion or a summary, it's a precise, literal instruction, and the recipe expects it to be followed exactly.

Recipes can also branch ("if using a metal pan, reduce the temperature by 25 degrees") and repeat ("knead the dough for 10 minutes"). Sound familiar?

Conditionals and loops again. The parallel isn't perfect, real recipes lean on human judgment and experience in a way code never will, but it's a useful mental anchor for what's coming in the next several chapters.

## Instructions Operate on Data

Instructions rarely do anything in isolation. They operate on data: numbers, text, true/false values, and more complex collections of these things. A program without data to act on doesn't do much of anything interesting.

This is where the next chapter picks up: before a program can meaningfully branch, loop, or calculate anything, it needs a way to store and refer to the data it's working with. That's what variables and types are for.

*"I told it to spread the peanut butter. I didn't tell it to stop."*

## The Core Idea to Carry Forward

If there's one idea to hold onto from this chapter, it's this: a program is nothing more than a precise, ordered sequence of instructions operating on data, executed by a machine that will do exactly what it's told, no more and no less. Every concept from here forward, types, conditionals, loops, functions, objects, is a tool for organizing and controlling that sequence more effectively. None of it changes the fundamental nature of what's happening underneath.

# Chapter 3: Input & Output Basics

## Why Start Here

Before diving into variables, types, and logic, it's worth pausing on something simpler and easier to overlook: how a program talks to the outside world at all. Every program, no matter how complex, eventually needs to take something in and put something out. Without that, it's just instructions running in isolation, invisible to the person who wrote them.

This chapter covers the simplest form of that conversation: the console.

## Output: The Simplest Form of Communication

Output is anything a program produces and makes visible, most commonly, at this basic level, as text printed to a console or terminal window.

Nearly every language has some version of a "print" statement. It might look like:

```
print("Hello, world!")
```

or

```
console.log("Hello, world!")
```

or

```
System.out.println("Hello, world!");
```

The exact syntax differs, but the idea is identical across every language you'll ever encounter: take this piece of data, and display it somewhere the person running the program can see it.

This is, famously, the first program most people ever write, and for good reason. It's the simplest possible proof that a program ran, and that it can communicate something back.

## Input: Getting Data From the Outside

Input is the reverse: a way for the program to receive information from outside itself, most simply, by asking the person running it to type something.

```
name = input("What's your name?")
```

This single line does something worth pausing on. It pauses the program's execution, waits for a person to type a response, and stores whatever they typed so the program can use it later. That "stores it for later" detail is really a preview of the next chapter: whatever the person types has to go somewhere, and that somewhere is a variable.

## The Console as a Two-Way Conversation

Put input and output together, and you get the simplest possible interactive program:

```
name = input("What's your name?")
print("Hello, " + name + "!")
```

This is a genuine conversation, however basic. The program asks a question, waits, listens, and responds using what it heard. Every chatbot, every command-line tool, every form on a website is, underneath all its complexity, built on this same basic pattern repeated many times over.

## Beyond the Console

The console is the simplest form of I/O, but it's worth knowing, even at this early stage, that it's far from the only one. Programs can also receive input from files, databases, sensors, network requests, or other programs, and can send output to screens, files, printers, or across a network to another machine entirely.

None of that changes the underlying idea. Input is data coming in; output is data going out. The console is simply the most direct and least complicated way to see that happening, which is exactly why it's the right place to start.

## Why This Comes Before Types and Logic

It might seem like input and output should come later, after the more foundational-feeling concepts like variables and conditionals. But there's a good reason to introduce it first: every example in the chapters that follow will need a way to show its results. Rather than treating "print this out" as a mysterious piece of magic borrowed from later material, it's better to understand it now, so it can be used freely, and without confusion, as a tool throughout the rest of this book.

## Looking Ahead

The next chapter picks up on the thread this one left dangling: when a program receives input, or needs to hold onto any piece of data at all, it needs somewhere to put it, and a way to know what kind of thing it's holding. That's the subject of variables and types.

# Chapter 4: Variables & Types

## Giving Data a Name

In the last chapter, a program asked a question and had to "store it for later." That storage mechanism is a variable: a named place to keep a piece of data so the program can refer to it again, use it in calculations, or change it as execution continues.

```
age = 34
```

Here, age is the name, and 34 is the value it currently holds. From this point on, the program can use age anywhere it needs that value, without having to know or care what the number actually is. That's the entire point of a variable: it lets code refer to data by a meaningful name instead of a literal value, which makes programs both easier to write and dramatically easier to read.

## Why "Variable" Is the Right Word

The name is well chosen, because the value a variable holds can vary over time.

```
age = 34
age = 35
```

After the second line, age holds 35. The old value is gone, replaced. This is one of the most fundamental behaviors in programming: a variable is a container, not a fixed label, and what's inside that container can change as the program runs.

## Types: What Kind of Data Is This?

Not all data is the same, and most languages want to know, in some form, what type of data a variable is holding. The three most fundamental types, present in essentially every programming language ever created, are:

Numbers. Values you can do arithmetic with. Most languages further split these into integers (whole numbers, like 34) and floating-point numbers

(numbers with a decimal point, like 34.5).

Strings. Text, usually written as string literals inside quotation marks, like "Bob" or "hello, world". Some languages treat a single character as a string of length one; others provide a separate character type for it.

Booleans. A value that is only ever true or false. Named after George Boole, whose 19th-century work on logic underpins how computers make decisions.

```
age = 34               // number
name = "Bob"           // string
isEmployed = true      // boolean
```

(The // marks a comment, a note left for the human reader that the program itself ignores entirely. More on these in Chapter 22.)

Types matter because they determine what operations make sense. Adding two numbers is obvious. Adding two strings usually means joining them together, "Bob" + " Johnson" becomes "Bob Johnson", which is a completely different operation wearing the same + symbol. Trying to add a number to a boolean, meanwhile, is the kind of thing that causes real confusion, and different languages handle it differently, some refusing outright, some making an assumption on your behalf.

## Naming Variables Well

A variable can technically be named almost anything, within a language's rules, but naming it well is a real skill, not an afterthought. Compare:

```
x = 34
```

to

```
age = 34
```

Both are valid. Only one tells you anything, six months from now, when you've forgotten exactly what this piece of code was doing. Good variable names describe what the data represents, not what type it is or how it's being used internally. This becomes more important, not less, as programs grow larger.

## Constants & Mutability

Sometimes a piece of data genuinely should never change once it's set: the number of days in a week, the value of pi to a given precision, a configuration setting loaded once at startup. For cases like this, most languages offer a way to declare a variable as a constant, sometimes using keywords like const, final, or readonly.

```
const daysInWeek = 7
```

Attempting to reassign a constant after it's been set is typically treated as an error, one the language catches for you rather than one you discover by accident three functions later.

Declaring something as constant isn't just a technical restriction, it's a form of communication. It tells anyone reading the code, including a future version of yourself, "this value is not meant to change, and if you see it changing somewhere, that's a bug." This idea, that some things vary and some things deliberately don't, is called mutability (or, in the constant's case, immutability), and it's a concept that reappears throughout this book, particularly when strings are covered in detail later.

## Type Conversion & Casting

Data doesn't always arrive in the type a program needs it in. Recall the input example from the last chapter:

```
age = input("How old are you?")
```

Whatever the person types is very often received as a string, even if they type 34, because keyboards produce text and the program has to make a deliberate choice to treat that text as a number. This is where type conversion (also called casting) comes in: explicitly telling the program to reinterpret a piece of data as a different type.

```
age = input("How old are you?")      // "34", a string
age = toNumber(age)                   // 34, a number
```

Some conversions are safe and obvious, like turning "34" into 34. Others are lossy or ambiguous, turning 34.9 into an integer loses the .9 entirely, and turning "thirty-four" into a number doesn't work at all. Some languages perform certain conversions automatically, silently, behind the scenes, this is called implicit conversion. Others require it to be spelled out explicitly every time. Neither approach is strictly better, but knowing which one a given language uses is essential to avoiding subtle, hard-to-spot bugs.

## The Foundation Everything Else Builds On

Variables and types feel almost too simple to dwell on, and yet nearly every bug a programmer encounters, at every level of experience, traces back in some way to a misunderstanding about what value a variable actually holds, or what type it actually is. Getting genuinely comfortable with this chapter pays off for the rest of the book, and for the rest of a programming career.

## Looking Ahead

With data safely stored and typed, the next question is what a program can actually do with it. The next chapter introduces operators and expressions, the tools programs use to calculate, compare, and transform values.

# Chapter 5: Operators & Expressions

## From Data to Action

Variables give a program somewhere to store data. Operators give it a way to do something with that data. An operator is a symbol that performs an operation, usually on one or two pieces of data, and produces a result. Put a few operators and variables together, and you get an expression: a piece of code that evaluates down to a single value.

```
total = price + tax
```

Here, + is the operator, price and tax are the operands (the values being operated on), and price + tax is the expression. The whole line takes that expression's result and stores it in total. Nearly everything a program does, at some level, boils down to evaluating expressions like this one.

## Arithmetic Operators

These are the most familiar operators, largely unchanged from basic math class:

| Operator | Meaning | Example | Result |
|---|---|---|---|
| + | Addition | 5 + 3 | 8 |
| - | Subtraction | 5 - 3 | 2 |
| * | Multiplication | 5 * 3 | 15 |
| / | Division | 10 / 3 | 3.33... |
| % | Modulo (remainder) | 10 % 3 | 1 |

The modulo operator deserves a second look, since it doesn't show up much outside of programming. It returns the remainder left over after division. 10 % 3 is 1, because 3 goes into 10 three times, with 1 left over. This turns out to be surprisingly useful: it's the standard way to check whether a number is even or odd (n % 2 == 0), or to make something repeat in a cycle (a clock, a rotating list of colors, and so on).

One more subtlety worth flagging now, and revisited later: dividing two integers doesn't always behave the way you'd expect. In many languages, 10 / 3 doesn't return 3.33, it returns 3, discarding the remainder entirely, because both operands are integers. Getting the decimal result usually requires at least one of the operands to be a floating-point number. Other languages, including Python 3 and JavaScript, take the opposite approach, and produce a floating-point result from ordinary division even when both operands are written as whole numbers. This is a direct consequence of the types covered in the last chapter, and it's a classic source of quiet, hard-to-spot bugs, the lesson is to learn the specific division rules of whichever language you're using rather than assuming they're universal.

## Comparison Operators

Comparison operators compare two values and produce a boolean result, true or false:

| Operator | Meaning | Example | Result |
|---|---|---|---|
| == | Equal to | `5 == 5` | `true` |
| != | Not equal to | `5 != 3` | `true` |
| > | Greater than | `5 > 3` | `true` |
| < | Less than | `5 < 3` | `false` |
| >= | Greater than or equal to | `5 >= 5` | `true` |
| <= | Less than or equal to | `5 <= 3` | `false` |

Notice == uses two equals signs. This isn't decoration, it's a deliberate distinction from the single = used for assignment (age = 34). Assignment stores a value; comparison checks one. Mixing the two up, typing age = 34 when you meant to ask "is age equal to 34?", is one of the oldest and most common mistakes in programming, common enough that many languages and code editors now specifically warn about it.

## Boolean (Logical) Operators

Where comparison operators produce a single true/false result, boolean operators combine multiple true/false values into one:

<table>
<tr><th>Operator</th><th>Meaning</th><th>Example</th><th>Result</th></tr>
<tr><td>AND (often &&)</td><td>True only if both sides are true</td><td>true && false</td><td>false</td></tr>
<tr><td>OR (often ||)</td><td>True if either side is true</td><td>true || false</td><td>true</td></tr>
<tr><td>NOT (often !)</td><td>Flips a value</td><td>!true</td><td>false</td></tr>
</table>

These become essential the moment a decision depends on more than one condition. "Let this person in if they're an employee AND it's before 6pm" needs exactly this kind of combination, and it's a direct preview of the next chapter, where these boolean results are used to actually control what a program does.

## Expressions Can Nest

Expressions aren't limited to a single operator. They can combine, and even nest inside one another, exactly like a math expression can:

```
total = (price + tax) * quantity
isEligible = (age >= 18) && (hasID == true)
```

Just like in arithmetic, parentheses control the order operations happen in, and most languages follow familiar rules of precedence (multiplication before addition, for instance) even without them. When there's any doubt about how an expression will be evaluated, adding parentheses costs nothing and removes the ambiguity entirely, both for the computer and, more importantly, for the next person reading the code.

## Looking Ahead

Comparison and boolean operators exist for one purpose above all others: to let a program make decisions. The next chapter, conditional logic, is where that purpose finally gets used directly, letting a program choose which instructions to execute based on the very expressions covered here.

# Chapter 6: Conditional Logic

## Letting a Program Choose

Every program covered so far runs top to bottom, one instruction after another, with no deviation. That's fine for simple tasks, but it falls apart the moment a program needs to behave differently depending on circumstances. Should this user see an error message or a welcome screen? Should this order get free shipping or not? These are decisions, and conditional logic is how a program makes them.

At its core, a conditional does one simple thing: it evaluates a boolean expression (from the last chapter) and, based on whether that expression is true or false, decides which instructions to run.

## The If Statement

The most basic form of conditional logic is the if statement:

```
if (age >= 18) {
    print("You may enter.")
}
```

This reads almost exactly like English: if the condition in parentheses evaluates to true, the instructions inside the braces run. If it evaluates to false, they're skipped entirely, and the program continues on with whatever comes next.

This is the first real deviation from strict top-to-bottom execution introduced in Chapter 2. The program isn't guaranteed to run every line anymore. Which lines run now depends on data.

## Adding an Alternative: Else

Often, a decision has two sides: something should happen if the condition is true, and something different should happen if it's not. That's what else is for:

```
if (age >= 18) {
    print("You may enter.")
} else {
    print("Sorry, you must be 18 or older.")
}
```

Exactly one of these two blocks will run, never both, never neither. This is a genuinely useful guarantee: it means every possible outcome of the condition is accounted for.

## Handling More Than Two Outcomes: Else If

Real decisions frequently have more than two possible outcomes. Else if (sometimes written as a single keyword, like elif) lets a chain of conditions be checked in order:

```
if (grade >= 90) {
    print("A")
} else if (grade >= 80) {
    print("B")
} else if (grade >= 70) {
    print("C")
} else {
    print("Below a C")
}
```

This chain is checked from top to bottom, and the first condition that evaluates to true is the one whose block runs. Once one condition matches, the rest of the chain is skipped, even if a later condition would also have matched. Order matters here: if the checks above were reversed, checking grade >= 70 first, a grade of 95 would incorrectly stop at "C," since 95 is indeed >= 70. This is a genuinely common source of bugs, and worth internalizing early: conditions are checked in order, and the first true one wins.

## Nesting Conditionals

Conditionals can be placed inside one another, letting a program make a decision, and then a further decision based on the outcome of the first:

```
if (isEmployee) {
    if (hoursWorked > 40) {
        print("Overtime pay applies.")
```

```
    } else {
        print("Standard pay applies.")
    }
} else {
    print("Not eligible for pay through this system.")
}
```

Nesting is a natural and often necessary tool, but it comes with a real cost: readability. Nest conditionals too deeply, three, four, five levels in, and code becomes genuinely difficult for a human to follow, even though the computer has no trouble with it whatsoever. Often, combining conditions with the boolean operators from Chapter 5 (&&, ||) can flatten what would otherwise be a deeply nested structure into something far more readable.

```
if (isEmployee && hoursWorked > 40) {
    print("Overtime pay applies.")
}
```

## A Note on Syntax Differences

The exact punctuation for conditionals varies more than almost anything else across languages. Some languages require parentheses around the condition; others don't. Some use curly braces to mark the block of code; others use indentation alone, with no braces at all. Some spell "else if" as two words, others as one.

None of this changes the underlying concept even slightly. Every single one of these languages is doing exactly the same thing described in this chapter: evaluating a boolean expression, and choosing which instructions to run based on the result. Once that idea is solid, adapting to any particular language's punctuation is a minor detail, not a new concept to learn.

## Looking Ahead

Conditional logic lets a program choose a path once. The next chapter, loops and iteration, is about repeating a set of instructions multiple times, often governed by the very same kinds of conditions introduced here.

# Chapter 7: Loops & Iteration

## Doing Something More Than Once

Conditionals let a program choose a path once. But a huge amount of what programs do involves repetition: processing every item in a list, checking a condition again and again until something changes, printing a message ten times, reading every line of a file. Writing the same instructions out by hand ten, a hundred, or a million times isn't practical. Loops solve this by letting a set of instructions repeat, automatically, as many times as needed.

This is the second way, alongside conditionals, that a program deviates from strict top-to-bottom execution. Instead of skipping instructions, a loop goes backward, returning to an earlier point and running the same instructions again.

## The While Loop

The simplest loop is the while loop. It repeats a block of instructions for as long as a condition remains true:

```
count = 1
while (count <= 5) {
    print(count)
    count = count + 1
}
```

Before each repetition, the condition count <= 5 is checked. If it's true, the block runs, and then the check happens again. If it's false, the loop stops, and the program moves on to whatever comes after it.

Notice the line count = count + 1. This is what makes the loop eventually stop. Without it, count would stay at 1 forever, the condition would always be true, and the loop would never end. This is called an infinite loop, and it's one of the most common mistakes a beginner makes: writing a loop and forgetting to include the piece of code that eventually makes its condition false.

## The For Loop

While loops are general-purpose, but a huge number of loops share a specific, recurring shape: do something a known number of times, or do something once for each item in a collection. The for loop exists to express that shape more directly:

```
for (i = 1; i <= 5; i = i + 1) {
    print(i)
}
```

This produces exactly the same output as the while loop example above, but it bundles the setup (i = 1), the condition (i <= 5), and the increment (i = i + 1) into a single line, right where a reader would look for them. This is largely a matter of convenience and clarity rather than new capability. Anything a for loop can do, a while loop can also do, and vice versa, but for loops tend to read more clearly when the number of repetitions is known or easily calculated in advance.

Many modern languages also offer a variant sometimes called a for-each loop, designed specifically to step through every item in a collection without needing to manage a counter at all:

```
for (item in shoppingList) {
    print(item)
}
```

This chapter deliberately keeps that example brief. Collections are the subject of the next chapter, and for-each loops will make far more sense once arrays have been properly introduced.

## Controlling a Loop From the Inside

Sometimes a loop needs to stop, or skip ahead, before its normal condition would naturally end it. Two keywords handle this in most languages:

break exits the loop immediately, no matter what the condition says.

continue skips the rest of the current repetition and jumps straight to the next check of the condition.

```
count = 1
while (count <= 10) {
    if (count == 6) {
        break
    }
    print(count)
    count = count + 1
}
```

This loop is written to count to 10, but break cuts it short the moment count reaches 6, so it only ever prints 1 through 5. These keywords are useful, but worth using sparingly. A loop whose actual behavior depends heavily on scattered break and continue statements can become genuinely difficult to reason about, since the loop's real stopping condition is no longer just the one written at the top.

## The Danger of Infinite Loops

It's worth returning to the infinite loop problem once more, because it's one of the most common and most disruptive mistakes a new programmer will make. A loop with a condition that never becomes false will run forever, consuming the program's attention (and often the computer's resources) indefinitely, usually forcing the program to be forcibly stopped from outside.

Every loop should have a clear, verifiable path toward its condition eventually becoming false. When writing a loop, it's worth explicitly asking: what, exactly, changes on each repetition that will eventually make this stop? If there's no good answer, that's worth stopping and reconsidering before running the code at all.

## Looking Ahead

Loops become far more useful once there's a natural collection of things to loop over, rather than just a counted range of numbers. The next chapter introduces arrays and collections, and revisits the for-each loop from earlier in this chapter with real data behind it.

# Chapter 8: Arrays & Collections

## More Than One Value

Every variable so far has held a single value: one number, one string, one boolean. But most real problems involve groups of things: a list of names, a set of scores, a shopping list, a week's worth of temperatures. Storing each of those in its own separate variable would be unworkable.

```
score1 = 90
score2 = 85
score3 = 78
```

This falls apart almost immediately. What happens with a hundred scores? What happens when the number of scores isn't known in advance? Arrays exist to solve exactly this problem.

## What an Array Is

An array is a single variable that holds an ordered collection of values, all accessible through one name.

```
scores = [90, 85, 78]
```

Instead of three separate variables, there's one: scores, holding three values in a specific order. That order is preserved, and it's what makes arrays useful for far more than just storage. It means the values can be counted, stepped through in sequence, and referred to by position.

## Indexing

Each value in an array has a position, called an index, and that index is used to access a specific value directly.

```
scores = [90, 85, 78]
print(scores[0])   // 90
print(scores[1])   // 85
print(scores[2])   // 78
```

The detail that trips up nearly every beginner at some point: indexing starts at 0, not 1, in the vast majority of programming languages. The first item is at index 0, the second at index 1, and so on. This isn't arbitrary; it reflects how the position is calculated internally (as an offset from the start of the array), but it takes real, deliberate practice to stop reflexively counting from one.

Trying to access an index that doesn't exist, scores[10] on an array with only three values, is a common source of errors, and different languages handle it differently: some throw an error immediately, others return a special "nothing here" value.

*"In my defense, I started counting from zero."*

## Looping Through an Array

Recall the for-each loop introduced briefly in the last chapter. This is where it becomes genuinely useful:

```
for (score in scores) {
    print(score)
```

```
}
```

This steps through every value in scores, one at a time, without needing to manage an index or a counter manually. It's the most common way arrays and loops are used together, and it reads almost exactly like the underlying intent: "for each score in this collection, do something with it."

The traditional for loop from the last chapter also works, and is useful when the index itself matters, for instance, when comparing an item to its neighbor:

```
for (i = 0; i < 3; i = i + 1) {
    print(scores[i])
}
```

## Arrays Can Change

Arrays and array-like collections can generally have their existing contents changed after creation. Whether they can also grow or shrink depends on the language: some use fixed-size arrays and reach for a separate structure, often called a list, vector, or dynamic array, when resizing is needed.

```
scores = [90, 85, 78]
scores[0] = 95          // change the first value
scores.add(100)          // available on resizable array-like
collections
```

This is a meaningfully different behavior from the immutable strings covered in the next chapter, and it's worth flagging now so the contrast lands clearly later: arrays, in most languages, are mutable, at least in their existing contents. The collection itself can be modified in place, rather than requiring an entirely new array to reflect a change.

## Maps & Dictionaries: Key-Value Collections

Arrays organize data by position: first, second, third. But sometimes data is more naturally organized by a meaningful label rather than a position. A map (also called a dictionary, depending on the language) stores values associated with a key, rather than a numeric index.

```
person = {
```

```
    "name": "Bob",
    "role": "Engineering Manager",
    "age": 34
}

print(person["name"])   // Bob
```

Instead of remembering that the name happens to live at position 0, the code simply asks for "name" directly. This tends to be a far more natural fit for real-world data, where information is more meaningfully described by a label than by its order.

## Sets: Collections Without Duplicates

A set is a specialized collection with one particular, defining rule: it holds only unique values. Adding a value that already exists in the set has no effect, since it's already there.

```
uniqueVisitors = {"Bob", "Nancy", "Bob"}
// effectively becomes {"Bob", "Nancy"}
```

Sets are less commonly reached for than arrays or maps, but they solve a specific, recurring problem well: any time "does this list contain duplicates?" or "give me only the distinct values" comes up, a set is very often the right tool.

## Choosing the Right Collection

A short, practical way to decide between these three:

Order matters, and duplicates are fine → array

Data is naturally labeled, and you look things up by that label → map/dictionary

Only distinct, unique values matter, and order doesn't → set

None of these are mutually exclusive tools reserved for advanced programmers. They're foundational, and nearly every real program uses all three at some point, often within the very same function.

## Looking Ahead

Arrays and strings actually have more in common than they might first appear, a string is, underneath, a sequence of characters, not entirely unlike an array of them. The next chapter takes a close look at strings specifically, including a property that sets them apart from arrays: immutability.

# Chapter 9: Strings, Deep Dive

## A String Is a Sequence

A string, first introduced back in Chapter 4, is text: a name, a sentence, a single character, an empty line. But underneath that simple description, a string is really a sequence of individual characters, ordered, one after another, not entirely unlike the arrays covered in the last chapter.

```
name = "Bob"
```

This can be thought of as a tiny ordered collection: B, o, then b. That framing matters, because it explains why strings support some very array-like operations.

## Indexing Into a String

Just like an array, individual characters within a string can often be accessed by their position:

```
name = "Bob"
print(name[0])    // B
print(name[1])    // o
```

And, just like arrays, indexing starts at 0. The same zero-index habit from the last chapter applies here without exception.

## Measuring and Combining Strings

Two operations come up constantly when working with strings: finding out how long one is, and joining two together.

```
name = "Bob"
print(length(name))    // 3

greeting = "Hello, " + name
print(greeting)          // "Hello, Bob"
```

That + deserves a second look, since it's the exact same symbol used for arithmetic addition back in Chapter 5. Applied to two strings, it doesn't add in the numeric sense; it concatenates, joining them end to end into a new, longer string. This is a good early example of an idea that recurs throughout programming: the same symbol can mean genuinely different things depending on the types of data it's applied to.

## Why Strings Are Immutable

Here's where strings meaningfully diverge from arrays. In most languages, once a string is created, its individual characters cannot be changed in place.

```
name = "Bob"
name[0] = "T"    // typically an error, or simply not allowed
```

This might seem like an arbitrary restriction, but it's a deliberate design choice, made for a few genuinely good reasons:

Safety. If a string could be silently changed in place, any other part of a program holding onto what it believed was the same, unchanging piece of text could suddenly find that text altered underneath it, without warning.

Sharing. Many languages allow multiple variables to point at the same underlying string in memory as an optimization, rather than duplicating it. That optimization is only safe if the string can't change, since a change through one variable would otherwise unexpectedly affect the other.

Hashing and caching. Strings are frequently used as keys in the maps introduced in the last chapter. This depends on a string's value staying fixed and predictable; a key that could silently change would quietly break the whole structure built around it.

## What "Immutable" Actually Means in Practice

Immutability doesn't mean strings can't be transformed, only that they can't be changed in place. Every operation that appears to modify a string is actually creating a brand new string and handing it back.

```
name = "Bob"
name = name + " Johnson"
```

After this runs, name refers to an entirely new string, "Bob Johnson". The original string, "Bob", still exists conceptually as it was created, unmodified; the variable name has simply been reassigned to point at a different, newly created value. This is a subtle but important distinction from an array being altered in place, and it's worth sitting with until it feels intuitive, since it explains behavior that otherwise looks confusing, particularly around performance. Repeatedly building up a long string piece by piece inside a loop, for instance, can be surprisingly costly, since each step is quietly creating an entirely new string rather than simply extending the old one.

*"We don't edit the stone. We just carve a new one."*

## String Formatting & Interpolation

Joining strings and variables together with + works, but it gets clunky fast, and it's easy to lose track of spacing and punctuation:

```
greeting = "Hello, " + name + "! You are " + age + " years old."
```

Most modern languages offer string interpolation, a way to embed variables directly inside a string, without breaking out of it repeatedly:

```
greeting = "Hello, ${name}! You are ${age} years old."
```

The exact syntax for this varies quite a bit between languages, sometimes ${}, sometimes an f prefix, sometimes something else entirely, but the underlying goal is identical everywhere it appears: make it easy to read a string with variables embedded in it, closer to how it actually looks once printed, rather than having to mentally reconstruct it from a chain of separate pieces joined by +.

## Looking Ahead

Strings, arrays, and the values covered in earlier chapters have mostly been used inline so far, created and used within a single, short block of code. The next chapter introduces functions, which make it possible to package a set of instructions, like the ones covered throughout this book so far, into a single, reusable, named unit.

# Chapter 10: Functions

## Packaging Instructions for Reuse

Every concept so far, variables, operators, conditionals, loops, arrays, strings, has been used inline: written directly into the flow of a program, exactly where it's needed. But real programs often need to do the same thing, the exact same sequence of steps, in more than one place. Copying and pasting that sequence every time it's needed works, technically, but it creates a real problem: if that logic ever needs to change, every single copy has to be found and updated, and it's astonishingly easy to miss one.

A function solves this by giving a named, reusable block of instructions a single home.

```
function greet(name) {
    print("Hello, " + name + "!")
}
```

Once defined, this block of instructions can be run, or called, from anywhere else in the program, as many times as needed:

```
greet("Bob")
greet("Nancy")
```

Each call runs the exact same instructions, substituting in whatever value was passed along.

## Inputs: Parameters and Arguments

In the example above, name is a parameter: a placeholder variable the function expects to receive a value for. When the function is actually called, the specific value handed over, "Bob" or "Nancy", is called an argument. The distinction is subtle but genuinely useful: the parameter is the name used inside the function's own definition; the argument is the actual value supplied at the moment it's called.

Functions can take more than one parameter:

```
function greet(name, timeOfDay) {
```

```
    print("Good " + timeOfDay + ", " + name + "!")
}

greet("Bob", "morning")
```

## Outputs: Return Values

A function often needs to hand a result back to whatever called it, rather than simply printing something directly. This is done with a return statement:

```
function add(a, b) {
    return a + b
}

total = add(5, 3)
print(total)    // 8
```

The moment a return statement runs, the function stops executing immediately, and control passes back to wherever it was called from, along with whatever value followed the word return. Any instructions written after a return statement, inside that same function, simply never run; they're unreachable.

Not every function needs to return a value. A function like greet above exists purely for its side effect, printing something, and doesn't need to hand anything back. Languages generally have a way to represent "this function doesn't return a meaningful value," and calling code should generally not expect one when it does.

## Multiple Return Values & Tuples

Sometimes a single result isn't enough; a function might need to hand back two or three related pieces of information at once, a minimum and a maximum, for instance, or a name and an age together. Some languages allow returning more than one value directly:

```
function minAndMax(numbers) {
    return smallest, largest
}

low, high = minAndMax(scores)
```

Other languages accomplish the same goal by bundling multiple values into a single, lightweight structure called a tuple, an ordered, fixed-size group of values treated as one unit, then returning that tuple as the function's single return value. Either approach solves the same underlying problem: getting more than one piece of related information back out of a function, cleanly, without resorting to awkward workarounds.

## Why Functions Matter Beyond Just Avoiding Repetition

Avoiding copy-paste is a real benefit, but functions offer something arguably more important: they let a program be organized around what it's doing, at a glance, rather than forcing a reader to track every individual step.

```
processOrder(order)
sendConfirmationEmail(order)
updateInventory(order)
```

Even without seeing what's inside any of these three functions, their names alone tell a reader almost everything they need to know about what this part of the program accomplishes. This is sometimes called abstraction: hiding the detailed "how" behind a clearly named "what," so a reader (often the same person who wrote it, reading it again months later) can understand a program's overall shape without having to hold every low-level detail in their head simultaneously.

## Looking Ahead

Functions make programs easier to organize, but they don't yet address a critical question: what happens when something goes wrong inside one? A file that doesn't exist, a division by zero, input that isn't the type expected. The next chapter, error handling, covers how programs detect and respond to exactly these situations, gracefully, rather than simply crashing outright.

# Chapter 11: Error Handling

## When Things Go Wrong

Every chapter so far has quietly assumed that things go according to plan: the file exists, the input is a valid number, the network connection succeeds. Real programs can't make that assumption. Files go missing, users type letters where numbers were expected, network connections drop mid-request. Error handling is how a program anticipates that things might go wrong, and responds deliberately, rather than simply crashing the moment something unexpected happens.

## What Happens Without Error Handling

Consider a simple example: dividing a number by another number provided as input.

```
a = 10
b = 0
result = a / b
```

Dividing by zero is undefined, and most languages will treat this as an error, stopping the program immediately at that exact line. Without any handling in place, the entire program halts right there, and whatever it was doing, whatever the user was in the middle of, comes to an abrupt, ungraceful stop.

## Exceptions: Errors That Can Be Caught

Most modern languages handle this using a mechanism called an exception. When something goes wrong, the program throws (or raises) an exception, and normal execution stops immediately at that point, unless something has been specifically set up to catch it.

The most common structure for this is a try/catch block:

```
try {
    result = a / b
    print(result)
} catch (error) {
    print("Something went wrong: " + error)
```

```
}
```

The try block contains code that might fail. If it runs without any problems, the catch block is simply skipped entirely. But if an exception is thrown anywhere inside the try block, execution immediately jumps to the catch block instead, where the program gets a chance to respond, rather than crashing outright.

## Why "Failing Gracefully" Matters

The phrase "failing gracefully" comes up constantly around error handling, and it's worth unpacking exactly what it means. It doesn't mean errors are prevented, some things will always be genuinely out of a program's control. It means that when an error does happen, the program responds in a controlled, intentional way: showing a clear message, logging details for later, cleaning up any partially completed work, rather than simply stopping wherever it happened to be.

Compare a program that crashes with a cryptic, technical error message the moment a user types their age as "thirty-four" instead of "34," to one that catches that specific problem and responds with, "That doesn't look like a number, please try again." Both programs encountered the exact same underlying problem. Only one of them handled it well.

## Not Every Error Should Be Caught

It's tempting, once try/catch is available, to wrap enormous sections of a program in it, catching absolutely everything, just in case. This is generally a mistake. Catching an error means the program is claiming it knows how to respond sensibly to that specific problem. Catching an error it doesn't actually know how to handle well often just hides a real, serious problem, letting the program limp along in a broken, unpredictable state rather than stopping cleanly where the original issue could be seen and fixed.

A reasonable general principle: catch errors at the point where something meaningful can actually be done about them, showing the user a clear message, retrying a failed operation, falling back to a default value, and let errors that genuinely can't be handled well propagate up, rather than being silently swallowed and forgotten.

## Finally: Cleanup That Always Happens

Many languages support a third block alongside try and catch, usually called finally, containing code that runs no matter what happens, whether the try block succeeds completely, or an exception is thrown and caught, or even, in some cases, if the exception isn't caught at all.

```
try {
    openFile()
    processFile()
} catch (error) {
    print("Failed to process file: " + error)
} finally {
    closeFile()
}
```

This is especially useful for cleanup work, closing a file, releasing a resource, that absolutely must happen regardless of whether everything else went well or not.

## Looking Ahead

This chapter closes out Part I of this book. Every fundamental concept needed to write real, working programs, variables, types, operators, conditionals, loops, arrays, strings, functions, and now error handling, has now been introduced. Part II builds on this foundation, going a level deeper into how these fundamentals actually work underneath the surface, starting with how data is represented in binary at the most basic level a machine understands.

# Part II: Going Deeper

# Chapter 12: Under the Hood: Binary & Representation

## Everything Is Ultimately Binary

Part I covered numbers, strings, and booleans as if they were simply given, ready to use. Underneath every one of them, at the most basic physical level a computer operates on, there's no such thing as a number, a letter, or a word. There is only binary: a series of switches, each one either on or off, represented as 1 or 0.

This chapter goes one level below the fundamentals covered so far, into how the data from Chapter 4 is actually represented once it leaves the comfort of a variable name and becomes something a processor can act on directly.

## Bits and Bytes

A single binary digit, a single 1 or 0, is called a bit. On its own, a bit can only represent two states: on or off, true or false, yes or no. That's not very expressive by itself, but bits are never used alone. Group eight of them together, and you get a byte, capable of representing 256 distinct combinations (2 multiplied by itself 8 times).

Binary numbers work exactly like the familiar decimal (base-10) number system, just with only two digits available instead of ten. In decimal, each position represents a power of ten: ones, tens, hundreds. In binary, each position represents a power of two: ones, twos, fours, eights, and so on.

```
Binary:   1  0  1  1
Value:    8  0  2  1   =  8 + 0 + 2 + 1  =  11
```

So the binary sequence 1011 represents the decimal number 11. Every number stored in a computer, no matter which type it's labeled as at the language level, is ultimately just a sequence of bits like this one.

## Representing Negative Numbers: Two's Complement

Representing positive numbers in binary is fairly intuitive, but negative numbers raise a real question: how do you represent a "minus" sign using nothing but 1s and 0s? The near-universal answer used by modern computers is called two's complement.

The core idea: to represent a negative number, take the binary form of its positive counterpart, flip every bit (every 1 becomes 0, and every 0 becomes 1), and then add 1 to the result.

```
5 in binary (4 bits):     0101
Flip every bit:           1010
Add 1:                    1011    -> this represents -5
```

This might look like an unnecessarily roundabout way to represent a simple negative sign, but it has one major, deliberate advantage: it allows addition and subtraction to work using the exact same hardware circuitry, regardless of whether the numbers involved are positive or negative. The processor doesn't need any special-case logic for negative numbers at all; adding 5 and -5 in two's complement simply produces 0, using ordinary binary addition, exactly as it should.

This is also the underlying reason a type's range of values has a hard limit, and why that limit is usually asymmetric, allowing one more negative value than positive value (a range like -128 to 127, for instance, rather than -128 to 128). One of the available bit patterns is reserved to represent zero, and the specific mechanics of two's complement mean that reservation comes out of the positive side.

## Bitwise Operators

Since everything is binary underneath, most languages provide operators that work directly on individual bits, rather than on the number as a whole. These are called bitwise operators:

(You don't need to memorize these to keep moving through this book. The goal here is just to show that a language can reach past a number's ordinary value and operate on the individual bits underneath it.)

<table>
<tr><th>Operator</th><th>Name</th><th>What it does</th></tr>
<tr><td>&</td><td>AND</td><td>Result bit is 1 only if both input bits are 1</td></tr>
<tr><td>|</td><td>OR</td><td>Result bit is 1 if either input bit is 1</td></tr>
<tr><td>^</td><td>XOR</td><td>Result bit is 1 if the input bits differ</td></tr>
<tr><td>~</td><td>NOT</td><td>Flips every bit</td></tr>
<tr><td><<</td><td>Left shift</td><td>Shifts all bits left, filling with 0s</td></tr>
<tr><td>>></td><td>Right shift</td><td>Shifts all bits right</td></tr>
</table>

```
  0101   (5)
& 0011   (3)
------
  0001   (1)
```

These operate bit-by-bit, comparing each position independently, which is genuinely different from the boolean && and || operators covered back in Chapter 5. Boolean operators work on a single true/false value as a whole; bitwise operators work on every individual bit of a number, in parallel, one position at a time.

## What Bitwise Operators Are Actually Used For

At first glance, working directly with individual bits can seem like a low-level curiosity with little practical relevance to everyday programming. In truth, it shows up in a handful of specific, recurring situations:

Flags and permissions. A single number can compactly represent several true/false settings at once, one per bit, a technique still used in some file permission systems and configuration settings.

Performance-sensitive shifts. A left shift (<<) by one position is mathematically equivalent to multiplying by two, and a right shift (>>) to dividing by two, operations that can be extremely fast at the hardware level.

Low-level programming. Networking code, graphics, cryptography, and embedded systems programming frequently need to manipulate data at exactly this level of detail, packing and unpacking individual bits within a larger piece of data.

Most day-to-day application programming rarely touches bitwise operators directly. But understanding that they exist, and what they're doing underneath, demystifies a layer of computing that would otherwise remain a black box, and makes concepts like integer overflow and the type ranges from Chapter 4 make sense on a much deeper level.

## Looking Ahead

With a clearer picture of how data is represented at the lowest level, the next chapter returns to a topic first raised in Chapter 4: types. This time, though, it goes deeper, into the distinction between value types and reference types, and what that distinction actually means for how data is stored and shared while a program runs.

# Chapter 13: Value Types, Reference Types & Typing Systems

## A Question Worth Asking

When one variable is assigned to another, what actually gets copied? It seems like it should be a simple question, and for some types, it is. For others, the answer is genuinely surprising the first time it's encountered, and it explains a whole category of bugs that otherwise seem inexplicable.

```
a = 5
b = a
b = 10
print(a)    // still 5
```

This behaves exactly as expected: a and b are independent, and changing one has no effect on the other. But watch what happens with an array from Chapter 8:

```
list1 = [1, 2, 3]
list2 = list1
list2[0] = 99
print(list1)    // [99, 2, 3]  <- list1 changed too!
```

list1 changed, even though the code never directly touched it. This isn't a bug. It's the direct, predictable result of a distinction that runs underneath nearly every language: value types and reference types.

## Value Types: Copies of Data

A value type stores its actual data directly. When a value type is assigned to a new variable, or passed somewhere, the data itself is copied. The two variables become entirely independent from that point forward. Numbers and booleans are the classic example, which is exactly why the first snippet above behaved the way it did.

## Reference Types: Pointers to Data

A reference type doesn't store its data directly in the variable. Instead, the variable stores a reference, an address, of sorts, pointing to where the actual data lives elsewhere. When a reference type is assigned to a new variable, only the reference gets copied, not the data it points to. Both variables end up pointing at the exact same underlying data, which is why changing it through one variable is visible through the other. Arrays, and the objects covered later in this part of the book, are typically reference types.

```
list1 -----> [1, 2, 3]
              ^
list2 -------|
```

Both list1 and list2 point at the same array in memory. There's only ever one array here, and two separate signposts pointing at it.

## Why This Distinction Exists at All

This isn't an arbitrary complication; it's a deliberate tradeoff around performance and memory. Copying a single number is essentially free. Copying an enormous array every single time it's assigned or passed to a function would be enormously wasteful, especially if that array holds thousands or millions of values. Reference types allow large collections of data to be shared and passed around cheaply, at the cost of requiring real, ongoing awareness of who else might be looking at, or modifying, the exact same underlying data.

## Boxing & Unboxing

Some languages, particularly ones with a strict split between value types and reference types, occasionally need to treat a value type as though it were a reference type, for instance, storing a number inside a collection that's designed to hold reference types generically. This process is called boxing: wrapping a value type in a reference-type container so it can be handled uniformly alongside other reference types. Unboxing is the reverse: extracting the original value back out of its wrapper when it's needed as a plain value type again.

```
number = 5              // a plain value type
```

```
boxed = box(number)    // wrapped in a reference-type container
original = unbox(boxed)    // back to a plain value type, 5
```

Boxing and unboxing happen automatically in many modern languages, often invisibly, but they aren't entirely free; each one does a small amount of extra work behind the scenes. In performance-sensitive code, unnecessary, repeated boxing and unboxing is a genuine, if usually minor, source of slowdown.

## Static vs. Dynamic Typing

Separately from value and reference types, languages differ in when they check that a variable is being used with the correct type.

In a statically typed language, a variable's type is fixed, and checked, before the program ever runs, often requiring the type to be declared explicitly:

```
int age = 34
age = "thirty-four"    // caught as an error before the program runs
```

In a dynamically typed language, a variable's type isn't fixed in advance, and isn't checked until the program is actually running and that specific line executes:

```
age = 34
age = "thirty-four"    // perfectly legal; age simply now holds a
string
```

Neither approach is unconditionally better. Static typing catches a whole category of mistakes early, often before code is ever run, at the cost of more upfront declaration. Dynamic typing offers more flexibility and less ceremony, at the cost of some errors only surfacing later, while the program is actually running, sometimes in production, in front of real users.

## Strong vs. Weak Typing

A related but distinct idea is how strictly a language enforces its types during an operation. In a strongly typed language, mixing incompatible types tends to be flatly refused. In a weakly typed language, the language will often quietly attempt a conversion on your behalf rather than raising an error.

```
result = "5" + 3
```

In a strongly typed language, this is often rejected outright: a string and a number simply can't be combined with + without an explicit conversion. In a weakly typed language, this might silently succeed, commonly producing "53" by treating the number as text and concatenating, or occasionally 8 by converting the string to a number instead, depending entirely on the specific language's own rules. This is exactly the kind of quiet, unexpected behavior that makes understanding a language's typing rules genuinely worth the effort.

## Null & Nil: The "Billion Dollar Mistake"

Most languages have a special value representing "no value at all," commonly called null or nil. It's used to indicate that a variable, particularly a reference type, doesn't currently point to anything.

```
person = null
```

This concept was introduced in 1965 by Tony Hoare, in the design of a language called ALGOL W. Hoare later publicly referred to it as his "billion dollar mistake," because of just how many bugs and crashes it has caused across the entire history of computing since. The problem is straightforward to state: if any reference-type variable might, at any point, be null, then every single piece of code that uses it has to remember to check for that possibility first, or risk trying to use data that simply isn't there. Forgetting even one of these checks, somewhere in a large program, is one of the single most common sources of crashes across the entire software industry.

Many modern languages have introduced features specifically designed to reduce this risk, ways of explicitly marking whether a variable is allowed to be null at all, and requiring that possibility to be handled deliberately before the value can be used. This is a direct, ongoing response, decades later, to the exact problem Hoare identified.

## Looking Ahead

This chapter covered where and how data lives, and how strictly its type is enforced. The next chapter turns to a related question: how long a piece of data actually lives, and where, exactly, in a running program it can be seen and used at all.

# Chapter 14: Scope & Lifetime

## Where Can a Variable Be Seen?

Every variable introduced so far has simply existed, available wherever it was needed. In practice, a variable is only visible, and only usable, within a specific region of code. That region is called its scope, and understanding it explains a whole category of otherwise confusing errors: "variable not defined," even though it clearly was, just a few lines up.

## Local Scope

A variable declared inside a function, like the ones covered in Chapter 10, generally belongs only to that function. This is called local scope.

```
function greet() {
    message = "Hello!"
    print(message)
}

greet()
print(message)   // error: message is not defined here
```

message exists only inside greet. The moment the function finishes running, message disappears entirely, and any attempt to use it from outside that function fails, because it was never visible out there in the first place.

This isn't a limitation to work around; it's a deliberate and valuable feature. It means a function's internal variables can't accidentally collide with, or be disturbed by, variables of the same name used somewhere else in the program. Two entirely different functions can each use a variable called message, count, or total without any risk of interfering with one another.

## Global Scope

A variable declared outside of any function, at the top level of a program, has global scope, meaning it's visible from anywhere in the program, including from inside functions.

```
appName = "NutriTrack"
```

```
function printWelcome() {
    print("Welcome to " + appName)
}

printWelcome()    // Welcome to NutriTrack
```

Global scope is convenient, but it comes with a real, well-earned reputation for causing problems as programs grow larger. If many different parts of a large program can all read and modify the same global variable, tracking down exactly which piece of code changed it, and when, and why, becomes genuinely difficult. A common, hard-won guideline among experienced programmers: prefer local scope by default, and reach for global scope deliberately and sparingly, only when it's genuinely the right tool.

## Block Scope

Many modern languages narrow this further, down to block scope: a variable declared inside a specific block of code, like the body of an if statement or a loop, is only visible within that specific block.

```
if (age >= 18) {
    var status = "adult"
}
print(status)    // error, in many languages: status not defined here
```

Block scope is a further refinement of the same underlying principle as local scope: keep a variable's visibility as narrow as it reasonably can be, so it's simply not possible for distant, unrelated parts of a program to reach in and depend on, or accidentally interfere with, something that was only ever meant to be used in one specific, small place.

## The Stack and the Heap

Scope explains where a variable can be seen. A closely related idea, lifetime, explains how long the underlying data actually exists in memory, and this is where the stack and the heap come in, the two main regions where a running program's data lives.

The stack is a highly organized, fast region of memory, used primarily for local variables and for tracking which function called which. Every time a function is called, a new section is added to the top of the stack, and every time that function finishes, that section is automatically removed. This maps directly onto local scope: the data genuinely disappears, cleanly and automatically, the moment the function that owns it finishes running.

The heap is a much larger, more flexible region, used for data that needs to live longer than a single function call, or whose size isn't known in advance. The arrays and objects covered in this book, being reference types as discussed in the last chapter, typically have their actual data stored on the heap, with only a reference to that location kept on the stack.

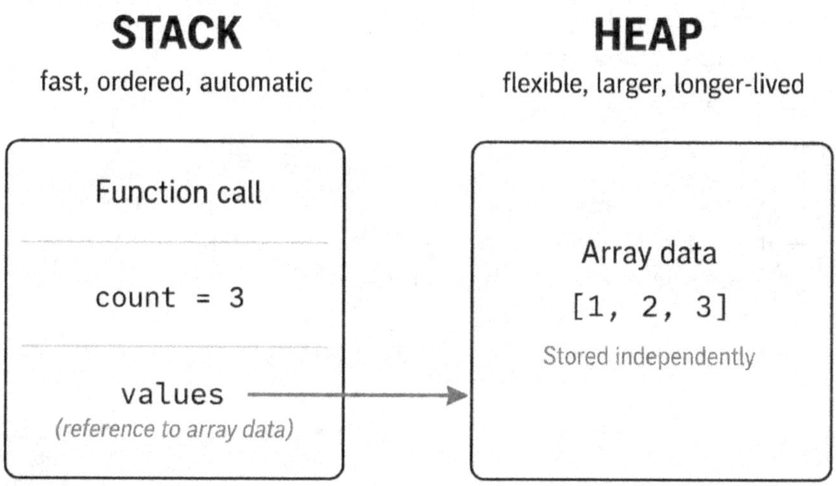


This stack-and-heap split is a genuinely useful model, but the exact physical placement of any one value is ultimately an implementation detail, and compilers and runtimes are free to optimize it differently than the simplified picture above. What matters most is the behavioral distinction underneath it: some data belongs to one specific function call and vanishes with it, while other data can keep existing for as long as something still refers to it.

## Why This Matters Beyond Trivia

Understanding the stack and heap isn't just academic background. It directly explains:

- Why local variables disappear the instant a function returns, but data referenced by an array or object variable can persist well beyond that.
- Why deeply recursive functions (covered in the next chapter) can eventually run out of stack space, an error commonly called a stack overflow.
- Why languages differ so much in how, and when, they reclaim heap memory that's no longer being used, the subject of memory management, covered later in Part II.

## Looking Ahead

Understanding how a function call adds a fresh section to the stack, and removes it automatically when finished, sets up perfectly for the next chapter's topic: recursion, a function that calls itself, and what that repeated stacking actually looks like as it happens.

# Chapter 15: Recursion

## A Function That Calls Itself

Chapter 7 covered loops as the standard way to repeat a set of instructions. There's another, quite different way to achieve repetition, one that doesn't use a loop at all: a function that calls itself. This is called recursion.

```
function countdown(n) {
    if (n <= 0) {
        print("Liftoff!")
    } else {
        print(n)
        countdown(n - 1)
    }
}

countdown(3)
// 3
// 2
// 1
// Liftoff!
```

countdown calls countdown again, with a smaller number, every time it runs, until it eventually reaches the point where it stops calling itself and simply prints "Liftoff!" instead.

## The Two Essential Pieces

Every working recursive function needs exactly two things, and missing either one is the source of nearly every recursion-related bug:

A base case: a condition under which the function stops calling itself and simply returns a direct answer. In the example above, that's n <= 0.

A recursive case: the part where the function calls itself again, but with input that's meaningfully closer to the base case than it was before. In the example above, that's countdown(n - 1), moving one step closer to zero with every call.

Without a base case, or with a recursive case that never actually gets closer to it, a recursive function calls itself forever, in much the same way a loop with a condition that never becomes false runs forever, covered back in Chapter 7. The consequence, though, is somewhat different, and worth connecting directly back to the last chapter: every recursive call adds a new section onto the stack, and since that stack has a limited size, an endlessly recursing function will eventually exhaust it entirely, causing an error commonly called a stack overflow.

## Tracing Through the Stack

Recursion becomes much easier to follow by connecting it directly to the stack and lifetime concepts from the last chapter. Each call to countdown adds a new section to the stack, and that section isn't removed until that particular call finishes completely, including waiting for any calls it makes to itself.

```
countdown(3)
  -> prints 3, calls countdown(2)
       -> prints 2, calls countdown(1)
            -> prints 1, calls countdown(0)
                 -> prints "Liftoff!", returns
            <- countdown(1) finishes, returns
       <- countdown(2) finishes, returns
  <- countdown(3) finishes, returns
```

Each level waits patiently for the call beneath it to fully finish before it can finish itself. This nested, layered structure is the essence of recursion, and it's precisely why deep recursion can consume so much stack space: every single layer of that structure occupies its own section on the stack, all at once, for as long as it takes the deepest call to finish.

## A Classic Example: Factorial

Recursion tends to shine brightest on problems that are naturally defined in terms of a smaller version of themselves. A classic example is the factorial of a number (written n!), the product of every whole number from 1 up to n.

```
5! = 5 × 4 × 3 × 2 × 1 = 120
```

Notice that 5! can be rewritten as 5 × 4!, and 4! as 4 × 3!, and so on. This is exactly the shape recursion is built for:

```
function factorial(n) {
    if (n <= 1) {
        return 1                    // base case
    } else {
        return n * factorial(n - 1)    // recursive case
    }
}
```

## Recursion vs. Loops

Any computation written recursively can also be written iteratively, and any repeated iterative process can generally be rewritten recursively, though converting a recursive solution to a loop sometimes means the program has to manage its own explicit stack to keep track of what recursion was handling automatically. Neither form offers a capability the other fundamentally lacks; the choice between them is generally about which one expresses the underlying idea more naturally, clearly, and efficiently.

Recursion tends to shine on problems that are naturally defined in terms of smaller versions of themselves, tasks like navigating nested folders within folders, or processing a tree-like structure where each branch looks like a smaller version of the whole tree. Loops tend to be the clearer, and often the more efficient, choice for straightforward repetition, like stepping through every item in the arrays from Chapter 8.

Recursion also carries a real cost that a loop doesn't: every recursive call adds another section to the stack, as covered above, while a loop generally reuses the exact same space on the stack, over and over, for every repetition. For problems that could be solved equally well by either approach, this makes loops the generally safer, more resource-efficient default choice, with recursion reserved for problems it genuinely fits better.

## Looking Ahead

Every collection covered so far, arrays, maps, sets, has held one thing after another in a fairly flat, straightforward structure. The next chapter looks at what happens when collections start containing other collections, arrays of arrays, and maps of maps, alongside a proper introduction to maps and sets themselves.

# Chapter 16: Maps, Sets & Nested Collections

## Revisiting Maps and Sets

Chapter 8 introduced maps and sets briefly, alongside arrays, just enough to know they exist and roughly when to reach for each one. With scope, lifetime, and reference types now covered, it's worth returning to both in a bit more depth.

## Maps: Looking Up by Key, Not Position

A map (sometimes called a dictionary, or a hash map) stores values associated with a key, rather than a numeric index like an array does.

```
person = {
    "name": "Bob",
    "role": "Engineering Manager"
}

print(person["name"])    // Bob
```

What makes maps genuinely useful, beyond simply being convenient, is how that lookup happens. A well-implemented map can find the value associated with a given key almost instantly, regardless of how many entries the map holds, whether it contains ten items or ten million. This is achieved through a technique called hashing: converting a key into a number, deterministically, and using that number to jump almost directly to where its value is stored, rather than checking every single entry one at a time in sequence.

This is also precisely why string immutability, covered back in Chapter 9, matters so much in practice. A key's hashed value has to stay fixed for as long as it lives inside a map. If a string used as a key could quietly change after being inserted, its hash would no longer match where it was actually stored, and the map would effectively lose track of it.

## Sets: Only the Unique Values

A set holds a collection of values with one defining rule: no duplicates. Adding a value that's already present in the set has no effect at all, since it's already there.

```
tags = {"urgent", "billing", "urgent"}
// effectively becomes {"urgent", "billing"}
```

Under the hood, a set is very often implemented using the exact same hashing mechanism as a map, just without bothering to store a separate value alongside each key. This is why sets share maps' major strength: checking whether a specific value is already present in a set is typically just as fast as looking up a key in a map, regardless of how large the set has grown.

Sets solve a specific, recurring class of problems especially well: removing duplicates from a list, checking membership ("has this user already voted?"), and comparing two collections for what they have in common, or what's different between them.

## Nested Collections

Every collection covered so far has held simple values directly: numbers, strings, booleans. But there's no rule limiting what a collection can hold, and a collection can just as easily hold other collections. This is called nesting.

An array of arrays is a common and natural way to represent a grid or a table:

```
grid = [
    [1, 2, 3],
    [4, 5, 6],
    [7, 8, 9]
]

print(grid[1][2])   // 6
```

grid[1] retrieves the second inner array, [4, 5, 6], and adding a second [2] retrieves the third item within that inner array, 6. Each layer of brackets steps one level deeper into the nested structure.

A map of maps is equally natural, and shows up constantly when representing real, structured data:

```
employees = {
    "bob": {"role": "Engineering Manager", "years": 5},
    "sam": {"role": "Dev Team Lead", "years": 3}
}

print(employees["bob"]["role"])   // Engineering Manager
```

This pattern, a collection whose values are themselves collections, is exactly how most structured data (configuration files, information retrieved from a database, data exchanged between two different programs) tends to be represented in practice. Nearly every JSON document, a format used constantly across modern software, is fundamentally just nested maps and arrays like these, stacked as deeply as the data actually requires.

## Looping Through Nested Collections

Looping through a nested collection generally means nesting the loops themselves, one level of looping for each level of nesting:

```
for (row in grid) {
    for (value in row) {
        print(value)
    }
}
```

The outer loop steps through each inner array in turn; the inner loop then steps through each individual value within that specific inner array. This mirrors the nested conditionals covered back in Chapter 6, and carries the exact same readability caution: nesting loops two levels deep is common and generally reads fine, but nesting much further than that is often a signal that the underlying data, or the logic operating on it, might be worth restructuring into something more manageable.

## Looking Ahead

Nested collections show that data can point to other data. The next chapter makes that idea fully explicit, introducing pointers and references directly, the underlying mechanism that's been quietly at work behind reference types since Chapter 13.

# Chapter 17: Pointers & References

## Making the Arrow Explicit

Back in Chapter 13, reference types were described using a simple diagram: a variable pointing at data stored elsewhere, rather than holding that data directly. That "pointing at" was left somewhat abstract on purpose, since the goal at the time was just to explain the resulting behavior. This chapter makes that arrow fully explicit, by introducing the concept directly underneath it: the pointer.

## What a Pointer Actually Is

Every piece of data stored in a running program lives somewhere, at a specific location in the computer's memory. That location has an address, much like a house has a street address. A pointer is a variable whose value is simply that address, a number identifying where a piece of data lives, rather than the data itself.

```
value = 42               // stored at, say, memory address 1000
ptr = addressOf(value) // ptr now holds the number 1000
```

To get from the pointer back to the actual data it refers to, most languages that expose pointers directly use an operation called dereferencing: following the address held in the pointer to retrieve, or modify, whatever's actually stored there.

```
print(ptr)               // 1000 (the address)
print(dereference(ptr))    // 42 (the actual value at that address)
```

## Pointers vs. Reference Types

It's worth being precise about a distinction that's easy to blur: a pointer and a reference type, from Chapter 13, are closely related, but not identical. A reference type, as covered there, is a broader, higher-level concept: a variable that refers to data stored elsewhere, with the specific mechanics generally hidden from the programmer, managed automatically by the language itself. A pointer is a specific, lower-level tool for expressing that same underlying idea, one that exposes the raw memory address directly, and typically requires the programmer to manage it explicitly.

Languages like C and C++ expose pointers directly, as a first-class part of the language, giving the programmer precise, low-level control over memory addresses, along with full responsibility for using that control correctly. Most modern, higher-level languages, Python, JavaScript, Java, and many others, use reference types extensively underneath, but deliberately hide the raw pointer mechanics from the programmer entirely, handling the details of addresses and memory automatically, out of view.

## Why Pointers Matter, Even If a Language Hides Them

Even in a language that never exposes a raw pointer directly, understanding what one is explains a great deal of behavior that would otherwise seem mysterious:

- It explains precisely why the array-assignment surprise from Chapter 13 happens: both variables held the exact same underlying address, pointing at the exact same data, rather than each holding an independent copy.
- It explains why passing a large collection into a function, covered in Chapter 10, is cheap and fast: only a small address gets copied and handed over, not the entire, potentially enormous, underlying collection.
- It explains why null, from Chapter 13, is such a persistent, recurring problem: a pointer or reference that doesn't currently point anywhere meaningful is, quite literally, an address of nothing at all, and following it leads nowhere useful.

## The Dangers of Raw Pointers

In languages that expose pointers directly, a whole category of serious, historically significant bugs becomes possible, precisely because the programmer holds direct, explicit responsibility for memory addresses:

A dangling pointer points to memory that's already been freed or reused for something else entirely, since the data it once pointed to no longer exists in any meaningful sense.

A null pointer dereference attempts to follow a pointer that isn't pointing anywhere at all, generally causing an immediate crash.

Pointer arithmetic errors occur when calculations involving an address go wrong, pointing somewhere unintended, sometimes into memory the program was never meant to touch in the first place.

These specific categories of bugs are a substantial part of why many modern languages were deliberately designed to hide raw pointers from the programmer entirely, trading away a measure of low-level control in exchange for an entire class of serious errors becoming effectively impossible to write by accident.

## Looking Ahead

Pointers and references explain how data can be shared and pointed to. The next chapter turns to a different, but related, idea: functions that can themselves be treated as values, stored in variables, passed around, and referred to, just like the data covered throughout this book so far.

# Chapter 18: Closures & Anonymous Functions

## Functions as Values

Every function covered so far, back in Chapter 10, has had a name, defined once, and called by that name whenever it was needed. But in most modern languages, a function isn't fundamentally different from any other value covered throughout this book. It can be stored in a variable, passed as an argument into another function, and even returned from one. This idea, that a function can be treated as data, is central to this chapter.

```
greet = function(name) {
    print("Hello, " + name + "!")
}

greet("Bob")
```

Here, greet isn't a special, separate kind of thing; it's simply a variable, exactly like age or name from earlier chapters, whose value just happens to be a function.

## Anonymous Functions (Lambdas)

Once a function can be stored in a variable, a natural question follows: does it even need a name of its own at all? Often, it doesn't. An anonymous function, frequently called a lambda, is a function defined without a name, typically written inline, exactly at the point where it's actually needed.

```
numbers = [1, 2, 3, 4, 5]
doubled = map(numbers, (n) => n * 2)
```

Here, (n) => n * 2 is a small, anonymous function: given n, return n * 2. It's never given a name of its own, because it's only ever used in this one specific place, passed directly into map, a function that applies it to every value in the numbers array in turn. Writing this out as a fully separate, named function elsewhere in the code would work identically, but would arguably make the code harder to follow, separating the logic from the one place it's actually used.

## Closures: Remembering the Surrounding Scope

Here's where this idea becomes genuinely powerful, rather than simply convenient. A function, whether named or anonymous, can "remember" the variables that were in scope, as covered back in Chapter 14, at the exact moment it was created, even after the code that originally created it has finished running. This is called a closure.

```
function makeCounter() {
    count = 0
    return function() {
        count = count + 1
        return count
    }
}

counter = makeCounter()
print(counter())   // 1
print(counter())   // 2
print(counter())   // 3
```

By the rules covered in Chapter 14, count is a local variable, and should disappear entirely the moment makeCounter finishes running and its section of the stack is cleared away. And yet, clearly, it doesn't; each call to counter() correctly remembers the running total from the call before it. The inner function, the one actually returned by makeCounter, has formed a closure over count, causing that captured state to remain available for exactly as long as something still needs it, rather than disappearing the instant the function that created it returns. A runtime commonly does this by storing the captured state in the kind of longer-lived memory covered in Chapter 14, though the exact mechanics vary by language and implementation.

## Why This Matters in Practice

Closures aren't a niche or purely academic curiosity; they show up constantly in modern, everyday code, generally for one of two closely related reasons:

Private, protected state. In the counter example above, there's no way to reach in and directly modify count from outside; the only way to affect it is by calling the function itself. This is a lightweight, effective way of protecting a piece of data from being changed by anything except the specific, intended piece of code that owns it, an idea that will resurface directly in the next part of this book, when encapsulation is covered.

Customized, reusable behavior. Passing a small anonymous function into another function, exactly as the map example did earlier, is an extremely common pattern for briefly customizing what a general-purpose function does, without needing to write an entirely separate, fully named function every single time.

## A Note on Terminology

Different languages use different terms for closely related ideas here, and it's worth being able to recognize them as variations on the same underlying concept rather than entirely separate ones: lambda, anonymous function, arrow function, and closure are all terms that show up across different languages, sometimes referring to almost exactly the same thing, and sometimes drawing a finer distinction between the function itself (the lambda) and its ability to remember its surrounding scope (the closure). The vocabulary varies; the underlying idea, a function that can be passed around as a value, and that can remember the scope it was created in, remains consistent everywhere it appears.

## Looking Ahead

Functions that can be passed around as flexible, general-purpose values raise a natural next question: how can a single function, or a single piece of code, be written to work correctly across many different types of data, without writing a nearly identical version for each one individually? That's the subject of the next chapter: generics.

# Chapter 19: Generics & Templates

## The Problem of Writing the Same Function Twice

Consider a simple function that returns the first item in an array:

```
function firstNumber(list) {
    return list[0]
}

function firstString(list) {
    return list[0]
}
```

These two functions are, in every meaningful sense, identical. The only difference between them is the type of data they're written to expect: one for numbers, one for strings. In a statically typed language, from Chapter 13, this duplication can become a genuine, recurring problem, since the language wants to know, in advance, exactly what type a function is working with. Writing a nearly identical version of the same function for every single type that might ever need it clearly doesn't scale.

Generics (sometimes called templates, depending on the language) solve this directly, by letting a function, or an entire data structure, be written once, in terms of a placeholder type, and used later with whatever specific type is actually needed at that moment.

## Writing a Generic Function

```
function first<T>(list: T[]) {
    return list[0]
}

first([1, 2, 3])          // works, T becomes "number" here
first(["a", "b", "c"])    // works, T becomes "string" here
```

Here, T is a placeholder, standing in for "whatever specific type this happens to be used with." It isn't a real type in itself; it's a variable for a type, the same way age from Chapter 4 was a variable for a value. When first is actually called, the language figures out what T should be from the data provided, number in the first call, string in the second, and checks that everything inside the function remains valid and consistent for that specific type.

## Why Not Simply Skip Type-Checking Entirely?

A reasonable question at this point: if the goal is writing one function that works across many types, why not just use a dynamically typed language, from Chapter 13, and skip static type-checking for this function altogether?

This is precisely the tradeoff generics are specifically designed to avoid having to make. Generics preserve the full benefit of static typing, from Chapter 13, catching type-related mistakes before the program ever runs, while still allowing genuine, meaningful flexibility across different types. Passing an array of numbers into a generic function still guarantees, and enforces, that every value inside it really is a number; it simply doesn't require a completely separate, nearly identical function to be written for every single type that might ever be used.

## Generic Data Structures

Generics apply just as naturally to data structures, from Chapter 8 and Chapter 16, as they do to functions. A map, for instance, is naturally generic over two independent types at once: whatever type its keys are, and whatever type its values are.

```
ages: Map<String, Number> = {
    "Bob": 34,
    "Nancy": 32
}
```

Map<String, Number> reads naturally once broken down: a map, generic over two placeholder types, here specifically filled in with String for the key and Number for the value. The exact same underlying Map structure works identically well holding numbers, strings, or entire custom objects, from the next chapter, as its values, without a single line of the map's own internal logic ever needing to change.

## Constraints: Narrowing What a Placeholder Can Be

Sometimes a generic function needs to do more with its placeholder type than simply store and return it; it might need to compare two values, for instance, which only makes sense if the specific type filled in for that placeholder actually supports comparison in the first place. Many languages allow a generic placeholder to be constrained, requiring that whatever specific type fills it in must meet some minimum requirement.

```
function largest<T extends Comparable>(a: T, b: T) {
    if (a > b) {
        return a
    }
    return b
}
```

This reads as: T can be any type at all, as long as it's Comparable, meaning it supports being compared with >. This preserves the exact same core benefit covered above, one function working correctly across many types, while still ruling out, safely and in advance, any type for which the function's own logic genuinely wouldn't make sense.

(The pairing of Comparable with > above is a simplification for readability. Real languages vary in exactly how a constraint like this is expressed, some allow an operator like > directly, while others require calling a comparison method or satisfying a trait instead.)

## Looking Ahead

Generics let a single piece of code work across many types of data. The next chapter turns to a different, though related, way of organizing code around data: objects, classes, and structures, where data and the behavior that acts on it are bundled together as a single, cohesive unit.

# Chapter 20: Objects, Classes & Structures

## Bundling Data and Behavior Together

So far, data and the functions that act on it have been treated as separate things. A person's name and age might live in a map, from Chapter 16, while a completely separate function operates on that map from the outside. This works, but as a program grows, keeping data and the logic that belongs with it consistently paired together, by convention alone, becomes harder to manage. Object-oriented programming offers a different way of organizing code: bundling data and the behavior that operates on it into a single, cohesive unit.

## Structs: Grouping Related Data

The simplest version of this idea is the struct (short for "structure"), sometimes called a record: a way of grouping several related pieces of data together under one name, without necessarily bundling in any behavior at all.

```
struct Point {
    x
    y
}

origin = Point(x: 0, y: 0)
print(origin.x)    // 0
```

A struct is really just a more structured, purpose-built alternative to the maps from Chapter 16, well suited to cases where the shape of the data is fixed and known in advance, a point always has exactly an x and a y, for instance, rather than an open-ended set of keys that might vary from one instance to the next.

## Classes: Adding Behavior

A class takes this same idea and extends it, bundling data together with the functions, generally called methods in this context, that operate specifically on that data.

```
class Person {
    name
    age

    greet() {
        print("Hi, I'm " + this.name)
    }
}
```

Here, name and age are the data a Person holds, and greet is a method: a function that belongs specifically to this class, and that operates on the specific data of whichever Person it's called on. The word this (called self in some languages) refers to the specific instance the method is currently being called on, distinguishing "this particular person's name" from any other person's.

## Instances vs. the Class Itself

A class is a blueprint, a definition of what data and behavior a Person has. It isn't, by itself, an actual person. An instance is a specific, concrete object created from that blueprint.

```
bob = Person(name: "Bob", age: 34)
nancy = Person(name: "Nancy", age: 32)

bob.greet()       // Hi, I'm Bob
nancy.greet()    // Hi, I'm Nancy
```

Person is the class, defined once. bob and nancy are two separate instances of it, each with its own independent data, name and age, even though they share the exact same blueprint, and the exact same greet method, defined only once. This distinction, one class, many independent instances, is central to how object-oriented code is organized.

Recall from Chapter 13 that objects, like arrays, are generally reference types. This matters here directly: assigning bob to another variable copies the reference, not the underlying data, exactly as covered with arrays back in that chapter.

## Encapsulation

Encapsulation is the practice of bundling data together with the methods that operate on it, while also controlling, deliberately, which parts of that data are exposed to, and modifiable by, code outside the class itself.

```
class BankAccount {
    private balance

    deposit(amount) {
        balance = balance + amount
    }

    getBalance() {
        return balance
    }
}
```

Marking balance as private means it can only be read or changed from inside the class's own methods, deposit and getBalance here, not reached into and modified directly from outside. This mirrors the closures covered in Chapter 18, which achieved a similar kind of protection using a different mechanism entirely. The underlying motivation is the same in both cases: guaranteeing that a piece of data can only ever be changed through a specific, controlled, intentional path, rather than in some unpredictable way from anywhere in the program.

## Enumerations: Naming a Fixed Set of Values

An enumeration, or enum, is a type that represents a fixed, specific, named set of possible values, and nothing beyond that set.

```
enum DayOfWeek {
    Monday, Tuesday, Wednesday, Thursday, Friday, Saturday, Sunday
}

today = DayOfWeek.Thursday
```

Compare this to representing the same idea with a plain string or number instead:

```
today = "Thursday"
today = 4
```

Both alternatives leave the door wide open to invalid values entirely by accident, "Thurday", misspelled, or 9, a day of the week that simply doesn't exist. An enum rules this out structurally, since today can only ever be one of the specific, named values the enum actually defines. This is a small feature, but a genuinely valuable one, for exactly the same underlying reason static typing, from Chapter 13, catches mistakes early: it turns a category of possible runtime mistakes into something the language itself refuses to allow in the first place.

## A Brief Note on Inheritance

Classes can also form relationships with one another, most commonly through inheritance, where one class is built directly on top of another, automatically gaining its data and methods, and then adding or changing some of its own. A Manager class, for instance, might inherit everything from Employee, and then add a few things specifically its own.

This is a genuinely deep topic, one that can easily grow into an entire chapter, or an entire course, by itself, covering ideas like polymorphism and interfaces. In keeping with this book's core goal, staying focused on the fundamentals shared across every language, this book deliberately leaves inheritance as a pointer toward further reading, rather than a fully developed topic here. What matters most for now is the foundation underneath it: structs, classes, instances, and encapsulation, exactly as covered in this chapter.

## Looking Ahead

Objects and classes describe how source code is organized and structured by the programmer. The next chapter turns to a different, related question entirely: how that carefully organized source code actually becomes something a computer can run at all.

# Chapter 21: How Code Becomes Execution

## From Source Code to Running Program

Every example throughout this book has been written in a readable, high-level form: variables with meaningful names, indentation, familiar words like if and while. Chapter 12 established that, underneath everything, a computer only ever executes binary. This chapter closes that gap directly, explaining exactly how readable source code becomes something a processor can actually run.

## Compilers: Translate Once, Run Many Times

A compiler is a program that translates source code, all at once, ahead of time, into a separate file containing machine code, or something very close to it. That translated file can then be run directly, as many times as needed, without the compiler needing to be involved again.

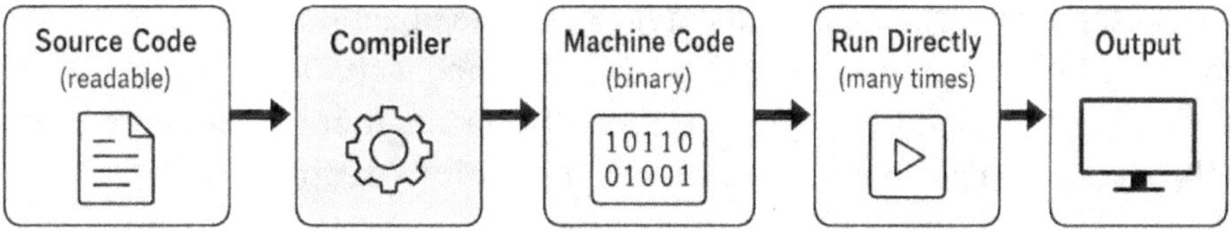


Chapter 1's history covered FORTRAN and COBOL as early examples of compiled languages, and C, C++, Rust, and Go continue that same tradition today. Compiled programs tend to run quickly, since all the translation work happened in advance, once, and the resulting program can be handed directly to the processor with no further translation needed. The tradeoff is a separate step, compilation, that has to happen before the program can be run at all, and a resulting file that's typically specific to the exact type of machine it was compiled for.

## Interpreters: Translate and Run, Line by Line

An interpreter takes a different approach entirely: rather than translating the whole program in advance, it reads and executes source code directly, translating and running each instruction, in turn, as it goes.

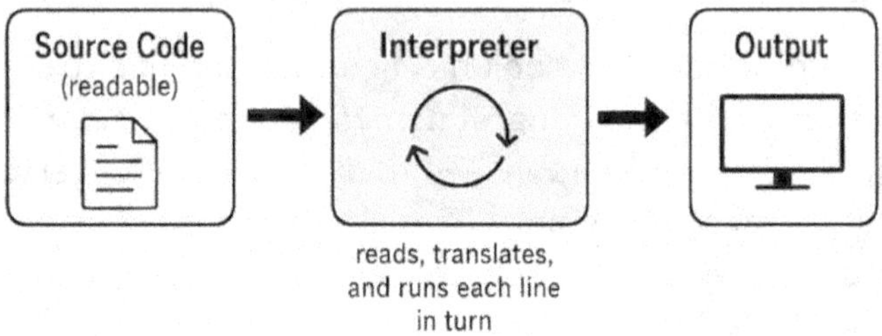


Python and Ruby are commonly cited as interpreted languages. Because there's no separate compilation step beforehand, interpreted code can generally be run immediately, without waiting on a translation phase first, which tends to make the cycle of writing and testing code faster and more immediate. The tradeoff is speed while actually running: since translation is happening continuously, on the fly, interpreted programs are typically slower to execute than their compiled counterparts. In practice, "interpreted" is more of a useful category than a strict boundary, the most common implementation of Python, for instance, actually compiles source code into an intermediate bytecode first, then runs that bytecode on a virtual machine, a pattern the next section covers in more depth.

## Somewhere in Between: Bytecode and JIT Compilation

Many widely used modern languages don't fit neatly into either category above, and instead use a hybrid approach. Java and C#, for instance, compile source code, but not directly into machine code specific to one type of processor. Instead, they compile into an intermediate form, often called bytecode, that isn't tied to any particular machine. That bytecode then runs on a virtual machine, a program that either interprets the bytecode directly, or, in many modern implementations, compiles frequently used sections of it into real machine code while the program is actually running, an approach called just-in-time (JIT) compilation.

This hybrid approach aims to capture real advantages from both sides: the portability of not needing a completely separate compiled version for every different type of machine, alongside much of the performance benefit that comes from genuine compilation.

## Transpilation: Source Code to Source Code

A transpiler is a distinct, related tool: instead of translating source code down into machine code or bytecode, it translates source code from one high-level language into another high-level language, one that's also meant to be read by a person, not just executed directly by a machine.

A common, everyday example: TypeScript, a language that adds static typing, from Chapter 13, on top of JavaScript, is transpiled into plain JavaScript before it actually runs, since browsers only know how to run JavaScript directly, not TypeScript itself.

Transpilation lets developers write in a language with genuinely useful features a target platform doesn't natively support, while still producing, at the end of the process, exactly the kind of code that platform actually knows how to run.

## Memory Management: Manual vs. Garbage Collection

Chapter 14 introduced the heap as the region of memory where longer-lived data, arrays and objects among them, actually lives. Someone, or something, has to eventually decide when that memory is genuinely no longer needed, and can be safely reused for something else. This is the job of memory management, and languages take one of two broad approaches to it.

In manual memory management, used by languages like C and C++, the programmer is directly, personally responsible for explicitly requesting memory when it's needed, and explicitly releasing it once it's genuinely done being used. This offers precise, fine-grained control, at a real, well-documented cost: forgetting to release memory causes a memory leak, where memory that's no longer actually needed is never given back, and slowly, gradually accumulates over the life of a running program. Releasing memory too early, meanwhile, while some other part of the program still needs it, produces exactly the dangling pointer problem introduced back in Chapter 17.

In garbage collection, used by languages like Java, Python, C#, and JavaScript, the language itself takes on this responsibility automatically. A separate part of the language's runtime, called the garbage collector, periodically checks which pieces of heap memory are no longer being referenced by anything the program can still reach, and reclaims exactly that memory automatically, without the programmer needing to request it directly. This removes an entire category of manual bugs, at the cost of some amount of runtime overhead, and a genuine, if often small, loss of precise control over exactly when memory gets reclaimed.

## Looking Ahead

This chapter closes out how code actually runs, underneath the readable syntax covered throughout this book. The next chapter turns to something more human-facing: how code is written, and formatted, so that it stays genuinely readable to the people who have to work with it, long after it was first written.

| Chapter 22: Code Style & Readability

## Code Is Written Once, Read Many Times

Every chapter so far has focused on what code does, and how a computer executes it. This chapter focuses on something different: how code reads to another person, or to the same person, encountering it again months later, having long since forgotten the specific details of why it was written a certain way. A piece of code is typically written once, but read, revisited, and modified many times afterward, often by someone other than whoever wrote it originally. Code that's technically correct but genuinely difficult to read imposes a real, ongoing cost, every single time someone else has to work with it.

## Comments: Explaining the Why, Not the What

A comment is text embedded directly in source code that the computer entirely ignores, meant purely for a human reader.

```
// Convert Fahrenheit to Celsius
celsius = (fahrenheit - 32) * 5 / 9
```

Good comments tend to explain why something is being done a particular way, especially when that reason isn't obvious just from reading the code itself, rather than simply restating what the code already says plainly.

```
// Bad: restates the obvious
age = age + 1   // add one to age

// Better: explains a non-obvious reason
age = age + 1   // birthdays count from the day after midnight
```

The first comment adds nothing at all; anyone reading age = age + 1 already knows it adds one to age. The second comment earns its place, since it explains a piece of context, a specific business rule, that genuinely isn't visible anywhere in the code itself.

## Naming Conventions

Chapter 4 briefly touched on choosing meaningful variable names over vague ones like x. This deserves a closer look, since naming well is consistently one of the highest-leverage skills in writing genuinely readable code.

A few durable principles that hold up across essentially every language:

Be specific. daysUntilExpiration communicates far more than d, or even days.

Match the convention of the language and codebase. Different languages have different established conventions for capitalization, camelCase in JavaScript and Java, snake_case in Python, for instance, and consistently following whichever convention is already in use matters more than which specific convention is chosen.

Name functions after what they do. A function called calculateTotal should calculate a total, and, ideally, do essentially nothing else beyond that; a function that does something entirely different from what its name suggests is actively misleading to anyone reading it later.

Avoid needless abbreviation. usrCnt saves a handful of keystrokes while costing a reader real, unnecessary effort figuring out what it actually means; userCount costs a little more typing and nothing at all in clarity.

## Consistency Matters More Than Personal Preference

Many genuine style debates, tabs versus spaces, where exactly a curly brace should go, how long a line of code is allowed to be, don't actually have one single, objectively correct answer. What matters far more than which specific choice is made is that a single codebase makes that choice consistently throughout. Code that mixes several different styles haphazardly is harder to read than code that consistently follows even a style an individual reader might not have personally chosen themselves.

Many languages and teams adopt a style guide, a documented, agreed-upon set of these conventions, and many also use automated tools, often called linters or formatters, that check or even automatically enforce that style, removing the need for constant, tedious manual review of purely stylistic choices.

## Keeping Functions and Blocks Small

Chapter 10 introduced functions partly as a tool for organizing code around a clear, nameable "what." That benefit erodes quickly if a function grows to do far too much at once, stretching to hundreds of lines and touching many, largely unrelated responsibilities.

A useful, durable guideline: a function should generally do one clear thing, and its name should accurately describe that one thing. If a function's name needs the word "and" to fully describe what it does, validateAndSaveAndNotify, for instance, that's frequently a real sign it should genuinely be split into two or three smaller, more focused functions instead.

## Readability Recurring Throughout This Book

Several earlier chapters have already gestured at this same underlying idea, from a few different directions:

Chapter 6 noted that deeply nested conditionals become genuinely hard to follow, and that combining conditions with boolean operators can often flatten and simplify them.

Chapter 16 noted the same caution applies to deeply nested loops.

Chapter 10 introduced abstraction, hiding a detailed "how" behind a clearly named "what," as a core reason functions matter at all.

This chapter draws those threads together into a single, explicit point: writing code that works correctly is necessary, but genuinely not sufficient. Code that works but reads as an impenetrable puzzle imposes a real, ongoing cost on every single person who has to maintain it afterward, quite often including the very person who originally wrote it.

## Looking Ahead

Style and readability matter within a single file. The next chapter addresses a closely related question at a larger scale: how code gets organized and divided across many separate files entirely, and how those files can rely on one another cleanly.

# Chapter 23: Modules & Imports

## Beyond a Single File

Every example throughout this book so far could plausibly fit in a single file. Real programs rarely stay that small. As a program grows, cramming every single variable, function, and class into one enormous file becomes unmanageable, difficult to navigate, and increasingly hard for more than one person to work on at the same time without stepping on each other's changes. Modules solve this by allowing code to be split across multiple files, each with a clear, focused responsibility, while still allowing those files to work together as a single, cohesive program.

## What a Module Actually Is

A module is simply a self-contained unit of code, generally corresponding to a single file, that can define its own variables, functions, and classes, and that can choose, deliberately, which of those things it makes available for other files to use.

```
// file: mathHelpers
function square(n) {
    return n * n
}

function cube(n) {
    return n * n * n
}
```

On its own, this file is just a normal collection of functions, largely indistinguishable from the code covered throughout the rest of this book. What makes it a module is the ability for another file to explicitly bring its contents in and use them.

## Importing Code From Another Module

An import is how one file requests access to code defined in another.

```
// file: main
import { square } from mathHelpers
```

```
result = square(5)
print(result)    // 25
```

The exact syntax for this varies considerably from language to language, some use import, others require, others #include, but the underlying goal is identical everywhere it shows up: take code that was defined somewhere else entirely, and make it usable here, in this file, without needing to copy and paste its actual definition.

## Why Not Just Put Everything in One File?

Splitting code across modules offers several genuine, practical benefits that become increasingly important as a program grows:

Organization. Code grouped by what it actually does, math helpers together, data validation together, network requests together, is dramatically easier to navigate than one continuous file stretching thousands of lines, with no clear internal structure at all.

Reuse. A module written once, mathHelpers from the example above, for instance, can be imported and used from many different files across an entire program, or even shared across several entirely separate programs, without ever needing to be copied or rewritten.

Collaboration. Different people can work on different modules largely independently, with far less risk of their individual changes conflicting directly with each other's work.

Encapsulation, at a larger scale. Chapter 20 covered encapsulation within a single class, controlling what data a class exposes to the outside world. Modules apply that exact same underlying idea at a larger scale, a module can choose to expose only a clean, deliberate, well-considered set of functions and classes to the rest of the program, while keeping its own internal, messier implementation details entirely private and hidden away.

## Namespaces: Avoiding Naming Collisions

As a program grows to include many different modules, it becomes increasingly likely that two entirely unrelated modules might independently choose the exact same name for something, two different modules each defining their own, unrelated function called validate, for instance. Many languages address this with namespaces, a way of grouping related code under a distinguishing prefix, so that two identically named things from different modules can still be told apart clearly and unambiguously.

```
mathHelpers.square(5)
stringHelpers.validate(input)
userValidation.validate(input)
```

Even though two entirely different modules each define something called validate, the module name attached in front makes it immediately, unambiguously clear which specific one is actually being referred to at any given point.

## Dependencies

When one module imports another, it's said to depend on it. A large, real-world program often has a substantial, layered web of these dependencies, with modules built on top of other modules, which are themselves built on top of still others, often stretching several layers deep. Managing this web well, keeping dependencies clear, well-organized, and reasonably shallow, is itself a real and significant skill, one that becomes increasingly important as a program grows from a small handful of files into hundreds, or even thousands, of interconnected ones.

## Looking Ahead

Organizing code well is necessary, but it's a separate question entirely from whether a given piece of code performs efficiently, or scales gracefully as the amount of data it handles grows. The next, and final, chapter of Part II offers a gentle introduction to algorithmic thinking, a light, practical look at how the efficiency of code itself can be reasoned about directly.

# Chapter 24: A Gentle Taste of Algorithmic Thinking

## A Different Kind of Question

Every chapter so far has focused on whether code produces the correct result. This final chapter of Part II asks a different, related question: how efficiently does it get there? Two pieces of code can produce the exact same correct answer while behaving completely differently as the amount of data they're working with grows, one staying fast, the other slowing to a crawl. Being able to reason about that difference, even at a basic level, is a genuinely valuable skill, and it builds directly on the loops and collections covered earlier in this book.

## A Motivating Example

Consider searching for a specific name inside an array of names, from Chapter 8.

```
function contains(names, target) {
    for (name in names) {
        if (name == target) {
            return true
        }
    }
    return false
}
```

If names holds 10 items, this loop checks, at most, 10 of them before finishing. If names holds 10 million items, this loop checks, at most, 10 million. The amount of work this function does grows directly, proportionally, alongside the size of its input. This relationship, between the size of the input and the amount of work required, is exactly what algorithmic thinking is concerned with.

## Introducing Big O Notation

Big O notation is a standard, shorthand way of describing how the runtime of a piece of code grows as its input grows, without getting bogged down in the exact, specific number of steps, which varies by machine, by language, and by countless small implementation details anyway. It focuses purely on the underlying growth pattern.

A few of the most common patterns, from fastest to slowest:

O(1): constant time. The amount of work generally doesn't grow with the size of the input. Looking up a value in a well-implemented map by its key, from Chapter 16, is a classic example, typically O(1) on average thanks to the hashing covered there, though collisions and other implementation details can affect the worst case.

O(n): linear time. The amount of work grows directly, proportionally, with the size of the input, n. The contains function above is a clear example: doubling the size of names doubles the worst-case amount of work required.

O($n^2$): quadratic time. The amount of work grows with the square of the input's size, commonly arising from a loop nested inside another loop, each one running across the same input.

O(log n): logarithmic time. The amount of work grows very slowly as the input grows, since each step effectively rules out a large portion of the remaining possibilities at once. A well-known example is binary search, covered below.

## Binary Search: A Concrete O(log n) Example

Imagine searching for a specific number inside an array that's already sorted, in increasing order. Rather than checking every value one at a time, as contains did above, a smarter approach is available: check the middle value. If it's too high, the answer, if it exists at all, must be somewhere in the first half; if it's too low, it must be in the second half. Either way, half of the remaining possibilities can be eliminated immediately, with a single comparison.

```
function binarySearch(sortedNumbers, target) {
    low = 0
    high = length(sortedNumbers) - 1
```

```
    while (low <= high) {
        middle = floor((low + high) / 2)
        if (sortedNumbers[middle] == target) {
            return true
        } else if (sortedNumbers[middle] < target) {
            low = middle + 1
        } else {
            high = middle - 1
        }
    }
    return false
}
```

Searching through 1,000 sorted values this way takes, at most, around 10 comparisons, since 1,000 can be cut in half roughly 10 times before reaching a single remaining value. Searching through 1,000,000 sorted values takes only around 20. This is the defining, genuinely remarkable characteristic of O(log n): the amount of work barely increases at all, even as the input grows enormously larger.

## Why This Matters, Even at a Beginner Level

This isn't purely an abstract, academic exercise. Understanding these patterns explains real, practical, everyday differences in how code actually behaves:

It explains precisely why looking a value up in a map, from Chapter 16, is generally so much faster than searching through an entire array for it.

It explains why a nested loop, from Chapter 16's caution about deeply nested loops, can quietly become a genuine performance problem once the data it's working with grows large enough.

It explains why sorting a list first, so that a fast search like binary search becomes possible afterward, is very often worth the upfront cost, particularly when that same list will be searched many times over afterward.

## A Light Touch, Deliberately

This chapter has intentionally stayed at a surface level. Algorithmic complexity, algorithm design, and formal analysis of runtime behavior are each entire, substantial subjects in their own right, well beyond the scope of a fundamentals-focused primer like this one. What matters most at this stage is simply the underlying habit of mind: noticing when the amount of work a piece of code does depends on the size of its input, and having at least a rough, working sense of whether that growth is likely to stay comfortably manageable, or eventually become a genuine problem.

## Looking Ahead

This chapter closes out Part II of this book. Every concept covered here builds directly on the fundamentals from Part I, going meaningfully deeper into how those fundamentals actually work, and behave, underneath the surface. Part III now turns to bringing everything together: a complete, end-to-end example using the concepts from throughout this book, followed by a tour of specific, real-world programming languages, both the classics and the modern.

# Part III: Putting It Together

# Chapter 25: Putting It Together

## An End-to-End Example

Every chapter in this book has covered one idea at a time, deliberately, in isolation, from variables through algorithmic thinking. Real programs, of course, don't work that way; they weave every one of these ideas together into a single, cohesive whole. This chapter closes out the conceptual material with one complete, worked example, pointing back to nearly every chapter along the way.

The task: build a small program that manages a simple, in-memory list of tasks, allowing tasks to be added, marked complete, and summarized. Deliberately modest in scope, but genuinely touching almost everything covered throughout this book.

(A quick note before diving in: the code below is language-neutral pseudocode, written to keep the ideas recognizable rather than to compile in any one specific language. A real implementation would need to adjust details like object construction, collection methods, and string interpolation to match whichever language you're using.)

## Setting Up the Data

First, a way to represent a single task, using a class, from Chapter 20:

```
class Task {
    title
    isComplete

    constructor(title) {
        this.title = title
        this.isComplete = false           // Chapter 4: a boolean,
defaulting                                       // to false
    }

    complete() {
        this.isComplete = true            // Chapter 20: a method
operating
                                   // on this instance's own data
    }
```

```
    describe() {
      // Chapter 9: string interpolation
        status = this.isComplete ? "done" : "pending"
     // shorthand for if/else (see Chapter 6)
        return "${this.title} (${status})"
    }
}
```

And a place to keep every task, using an array, from Chapter 8:

```
tasks = []   // an empty array to start
```

## Adding Tasks

```
function addTask(title) {
    newTask = Task(title)
    tasks.add(newTask)     // Chapter 8: arrays can grow
    print("Added: " + newTask.describe())
}
```

Calling addTask("Draft chapter outline") creates a new Task instance, from Chapter 20, and appends it to the tasks array. Note that tasks itself is a reference type, from Chapter 13; addTask doesn't need to return the updated array, since it modifies the exact same underlying array that already exists, in place.

(This example keeps tasks as a single global collection to stay compact, and every function below simply reaches out and uses it directly. That's a reasonable shortcut for a program this small, but Chapter 14's caution about global scope still applies: a larger program would generally do better passing the collection into functions explicitly, or placing it inside an object responsible for managing it, rather than letting many unrelated functions all reach into the same shared state.)

## Marking a Task Complete

```
function completeTask(title) {
    for (task in tasks) {                 // Chapter 7: a for-each loop
        if (task.title == title) {        // Chapter 6: a conditional
            task.complete()
```

```
            return true                    // Chapter 10: an early
return
        }
    }
    return false                           // Chapter 6: the task wasn't
found
}
```

This loops through every task, from Chapter 7, checking each one's title, from Chapter 6, and calling complete() the moment a match is found, before returning immediately, from Chapter 10, rather than needlessly continuing to check every remaining task afterward.

## Handling a Missing Task

```
function completeTaskOrWarn(title) {
    found = completeTask(title)

    if (!found) {
        print("No task found with that title.")
        return
    }

    print("Marked complete: " + title)
}
```

A missing task is an ordinary, foreseeable outcome, not a crash, so it's handled the way Chapter 6 taught: with a plain conditional checking the return value completeTask already gives back. Saving the exception-catching machinery from Chapter 11 for something genuinely capable of failing unpredictably, like the file access below, keeps that distinction clean rather than reaching for a try/catch just because one is available.

## Saving Tasks, With Real Error Handling

```
function saveTasks() {
    try {
        text = convertToText(tasks)
        writeFile("tasks.json", text)
        print("Tasks saved.")
    } catch (error) { // Chapter 11: a genuine, unpredictable failure
        print("Tasks could not be saved: " + error)
    }
}
```

Writing to a file is a much better fit for try/catch than a missing task ever was: the disk could be full, permission could be denied, or the file path could be invalid, none of which the program can rule out in advance. This is exactly the kind of exceptional, unpredictable failure Chapter 11's error handling exists for.

## Summarizing All Tasks

```
function summarize() {
    total = length(tasks)                    // Chapter 8
    completed = 0

    for (task in tasks) {
        if (task.isComplete) {
            completed = completed + 1    // Chapter 5: arithmetic
        }
    }

    print("${completed} of ${total} tasks complete.")

    for (task in tasks) {
        print("- " + task.describe())
    }
}
```

## Running the Whole Program

```
addTask("Draft chapter outline")
addTask("Write chapter 1")
addTask("Review with editor")

completeTaskOrWarn("Write chapter 1")
completeTaskOrWarn("This task does not exist")

summarize()
saveTasks()
Added: Draft chapter outline (pending)
Added: Write chapter 1 (pending)
Added: Review with editor (pending)
Marked complete: Write chapter 1
No task found with that title.
1 of 3 tasks complete.
- Draft chapter outline (pending)
- Write chapter 1 (done)
- Review with editor (pending)
```

```
| Tasks saved.
```

## Tracing the Fundamentals Through This Example

It's worth pausing to notice just how much of this book is actually present in that small, unassuming program:

- Variables & types (Ch. 4): title, isComplete, total
- Operators & expressions (Ch. 5): completed + 1
- Conditional logic (Ch. 6): checking titles, checking isComplete
- Loops & iteration (Ch. 7): stepping through tasks
- Arrays (Ch. 8): tasks, growing as tasks are added
- Strings (Ch. 9): interpolated summaries and descriptions
- Functions (Ch. 10): addTask, completeTask, summarize
- Error handling (Ch. 11): saveTasks, reserved for a genuine, unpredictable failure rather than an ordinary missing task
- Value & reference types (Ch. 13): why tasks didn't need to be returned
- Objects & classes (Ch. 20): Task, its constructor, its methods

Not every single chapter appears explicitly in this one small example, and that's expected; a modest task list has little natural need for recursion, generics, or bitwise operators. But this is precisely the point worth carrying forward: real, working software is built almost entirely from exactly this kind of combination, fundamental pieces, individually simple, brought together deliberately, rather than from some separate, more exotic body of advanced knowledge held in reserve.

## Looking Ahead

With every fundamental concept now demonstrated together in one working example, the final chapter turns outward, to the broader landscape of real, named programming languages, both the enduring classics and the current, modern favorites, and how the ideas covered throughout this entire book actually show up, in practice, across each of them.

# Chapter 26: A Tour of the Languages

## Reading This Chapter

Every language below gets the same short treatment: what it's for, one distinctive trait worth knowing, and a tiny snippet. None of these snippets need to be studied closely. The goal is simply recognition: seeing the exact same fundamentals from this book, variables, conditionals, loops, functions, wearing slightly different clothes from one language to the next.

## The Classics

### *COBOL (1959)*

What it's for: Business and financial data processing. Payroll systems, banking, insurance, much of the machinery still running large institutions today.

Distinctive trait: Deliberately English-like, verbose syntax, designed so that non-programmers could, in theory, read it directly.

```
IF AGE >= 18
    DISPLAY "You may enter."
END-IF.
```

### *FORTRAN (1957)*

What it's for: Scientific and mathematical computing. Still actively used in some high-performance scientific and engineering contexts.

Distinctive trait: One of the very first high-level languages ever created, predating structured programming itself, from Chapter 1.

```
IF (AGE .GE. 18) THEN
    PRINT *, 'You may enter.'
END IF
```

### *BASIC (1964)*

What it's for: Teaching programming to beginners; an early attempt to make programming approachable, sharing this book's own underlying goal.

Distinctive trait: Extremely simple, minimal syntax, designed explicitly for accessibility over power.

```
IF AGE >= 18 THEN PRINT "You may enter."
```

### *C (1972)*

What it's for: Operating systems, embedded systems, and any context demanding direct, low-level control over memory and hardware.

Distinctive trait: Exposes pointers directly, from Chapter 17, along with manual memory management, from Chapter 21, giving the programmer precise control and equally precise responsibility.

```
if (age >= 18) {
    printf("You may enter.\n");
}
```

### *Lisp (1958)*

What it's for: Symbolic computation, artificial intelligence research historically, and any domain valuing extreme flexibility in how code itself is structured.

Distinctive trait: Code and data share the same underlying structure, an idea that still influences functional programming techniques found in many modern languages today.

```
(if (>= age 18)
    (print "You may enter."))
```

## The Moderns

### *Python (1991)*

What it's for: General-purpose programming, widely used in data science, automation, education, and web development.

Distinctive trait: Prioritizes readability above nearly everything else; uses indentation itself, rather than braces, to define blocks of code.

```
if age >= 18:
    print("You may enter.")
```

### *JavaScript (1995)*

What it's for: The language of the web; runs natively in every browser, and, via additional tooling, on servers as well.

Distinctive trait: Dynamically and weakly typed, from Chapter 13, which grants real flexibility, at the cost of some genuinely surprising behavior around type conversion.

```
if (age >= 18) {
    console.log("You may enter.");
}
```

### *Java (1996, its first official public release; an early alpha had circulated in 1995)*

What it's for: Large-scale enterprise applications, Android development, and systems where portability across different machines matters greatly.

Distinctive trait: Compiles to bytecode, from Chapter 21, run by a virtual machine, prioritizing "write once, run anywhere" portability.

```
if (age >= 18) {
    System.out.println("You may enter.");
}
```

### *C# (2000)*

What it's for: Windows applications, enterprise software, and game development, particularly through the Unity engine.

Distinctive trait: Shares much of Java's philosophy and syntax, while adding a number of more modern, developer-friendly conveniences on top.

```
if (age >= 18)
{
    Console.WriteLine("You may enter.");
}
```

*Go (2009)*

What it's for: Backend and infrastructure software, particularly at large scale, where simplicity and fast performance both genuinely matter.

Distinctive trait: Deliberately minimal by design, intentionally leaving out several features (including some covered in this book) in favor of a simpler, more consistent language overall.

```
if age >= 18 {
    fmt.Println("You may enter.")
}
```

*Rust (2010)*

What it's for: Systems programming, in the same general space as C and C++, where performance and memory safety both matter a great deal.

Distinctive trait: Enforces memory safety, from Chapter 21, entirely at compile time, without needing garbage collection, through a distinctive set of rules called "ownership."

```
if age >= 18 {
    println!("You may enter.");
}
```

*Swift (2014)*

What it's for: Apple platform development: iOS, macOS, and related devices.

Distinctive trait: Combines modern safety features, including explicit, careful handling of null values, from Chapter 13, with a syntax designed to stay approachable for newcomers.

```
if age >= 18 {
    print("You may enter.")
}
```

## The Pattern Worth Noticing

Look back across all eleven of these tiny snippets. Every single one expresses the exact same idea from Chapter 6: check a condition, and print a message if it holds true. The punctuation shifts, sometimes parentheses are required, sometimes they aren't; sometimes braces mark a block, sometimes indentation alone does the job. But the underlying concept, conditional logic, never actually changes, not once, across sixty-five years and eleven genuinely different languages.

That consistency is the entire premise this book was built on. Learning any one of these languages well starts to feel, at that point, less like acquiring an entirely new body of knowledge from scratch, and more like learning the specific local vocabulary for ideas already deeply, genuinely understood.

## Closing

This book set out from a simple, honest premise: that learning to program had come to feel overwhelming, and that returning to the fundamentals, the ideas shared across every language rather than tied to any one of them, was the way back to solid ground. Twenty-six chapters later, from what a program actually is, through binary, objects, and algorithmic thinking, to this final tour across eleven real, working languages, that premise holds. The syntax in front of you will always keep changing. What this book covered doesn't.

## Where to Go From Here

You now have the conceptual vocabulary shared by nearly every programming language. The next step is to choose one language and start using these concepts in a real environment.

That next step doesn't only mean writing code yourself. Reading someone else's code critically, a colleague's, a codebase you're testing, or something an AI just generated, draws on exactly the same vocabulary.

Python is often a comfortable first choice, since its syntax stays close to the pseudocode used throughout this book. JavaScript is a natural pick for anyone interested in the web. C# or Java may appeal if class-based, strongly typed application development sounds appealing. C or Rust may appeal to anyone who wants to go further into systems and memory than this book did.

Whichever language you choose, you won't be starting from zero. As you meet each language's specific rules, it's worth deliberately mapping them back to what's already covered here:

- How does this language declare variables, and what types does it provide?
- How does it express conditionals and loops?
- What collection types are available, and how do they compare to arrays, maps, and sets?
- How are functions defined and called?
- How are errors represented and handled?
- How does it manage memory?
- The punctuation will be new. The ideas won't be.

# Glossary

This glossary covers the terms used throughout Underneath the Syntax, in plain language, with a pointer back to the chapter where each one is explained in full. Use it as a quick lookup, not a replacement for the chapters themselves.

Abstraction (Chapter 10). Hiding a detailed "how" behind a clearly named "what," so a reader can understand a program's overall shape without holding every low-level detail in their head at once.

**Anonymous function** (Chapter 18). See Lambda.

**Argument** (Chapter 10). The actual value supplied to a function when it's called, as opposed to the parameter name used inside the function's own definition.

**Array** (Chapter 8). A single variable that holds an ordered collection of values, each accessible by a numeric index.

**Assignment** (Chapter 4). Storing a value in a variable, written with =. Not to be confused with ==, which compares two values instead of storing one.

**Big O notation** (Chapter 24). A standard, shorthand way of describing how the runtime of a piece of code grows as its input grows, without getting into the exact number of steps.

**Bit** (Chapter 12). A single binary digit, either 1 or 0. The smallest unit of data a computer represents.

**Bitwise operator** (Chapter 12). An operator (**AND**, **OR**, **XOR**, **NOT**, and the shift operators) that works directly on the individual bits of a number, rather than on its value as a whole.

**Boolean** (Chapter 4). A value that is only ever **true** or **false**, named after George Boole.

**Boxing and unboxing** (Chapter 13). Boxing wraps a value type in a reference-type container so it can be handled like other reference types. Unboxing extracts the original value back out. Common in languages with a strict split between value and reference types, and not entirely free of runtime cost.

**Break** (Chapter 7). A keyword that exits the nearest enclosing loop immediately, regardless of the loop's own condition.

**Byte** (Chapter 12). A group of eight bits, capable of representing 256 distinct combinations.

**Bytecode** (Chapter 21). An intermediate form of compiled code that isn't tied to any one specific machine, run by a virtual machine rather than directly by a processor.

**Casting** (Chapter 4). See Type conversion.

**Class** (Chapter 20). A blueprint that bundles data together with the methods that operate on it. An individual object created from that blueprint is called an instance.

**Closure** (Chapter 18). A function that remembers the variables in scope at the moment it was created, keeping that captured state available even after the code that created it has finished running.

**Collection** (Chapters 8, 16). A general term for a structure that holds more than one value: arrays, maps, and sets are all collections.

**Comment** (Chapters 4, 22). Text embedded in source code that the computer ignores entirely, meant purely for a human reader.

**Compiler** (Chapter 21). A program that translates source code, all at once and ahead of time, into machine code or an intermediate form that can be run directly.

**Concatenation** (Chapter 9). Joining two strings end to end into a new, longer string, commonly using the + operator.

**Conditional** (Chapter 6). A statement, such as if/else, that lets a program choose which instructions to run based on whether an expression evaluates to true or false.

**Constant** (Chapter 4). A variable declared so that its value cannot be reassigned once set, communicating to future readers that the value is meant to stay fixed.

**Constructor** (Chapter 20). A special method that runs when a new instance of a class is created, typically used to set up its initial data.

**Continue** (Chapter 7). A keyword that skips the rest of the current loop iteration and jumps straight to the next check of the loop's condition.

**Dangling pointer** (Chapter 17). A pointer that refers to memory that has already been freed or reused for something else.

**Dictionary** (Chapter 16). See Map.

**Encapsulation** (Chapter 20). Bundling data together with the methods that operate on it, while controlling which parts of that data are exposed to code outside the class.

**Enum** (Chapter 20). Short for enumeration: a type that represents a fixed, specific, named set of possible values, ruling out invalid values by construction.

**Exception** (Chapter 11). An object representing an error, thrown when something goes wrong during a program's execution, and caught by a matching handler if one exists.

**Expression** (Chapter 5). A piece of code that evaluates down to a single value, typically built from operators and operands.

**Function** (Chapter 10). A named, reusable block of instructions that can be called from elsewhere in a program, optionally taking parameters and returning a value.

**Garbage collection** (Chapter 21). An automatic approach to memory management in which the language's runtime periodically reclaims heap memory that's no longer reachable, without the programmer requesting it directly.

**Generic** (Chapter 19). A function or data structure written once in terms of a placeholder type, then used later with whatever specific type is actually needed.

**Global scope** (Chapter 14). The visibility given to a variable declared outside any function, making it readable and writable from anywhere in the program, including from inside functions.

**Hashing** (Chapter 16). Converting a key into a number, deterministically, so a map can jump almost directly to where a value is stored rather than checking every entry in sequence.

**Heap** (Chapter 14). A large, flexible region of memory used for data that needs to live longer than a single function call, or whose size isn't known in advance. The exact placement of any one value there is an implementation detail rather than a strict rule.

**Immutability** (Chapter 9). A property of a value that cannot be changed in place once created. Strings are immutable in most widely used languages; any operation that appears to modify one actually creates a new string.

**Index** (Chapter 8). A number representing a position within an array, most commonly starting at 0 for the first item.

**Infinite loop** (Chapter 7). A loop whose condition never becomes false, causing it to run forever, usually a bug rather than intended behavior.

**Inheritance** (Chapter 20). A relationship in which one class is built on top of another, automatically gaining its data and methods and then adding or changing some of its own.

**Instance** (Chapter 20). A specific, concrete object created from a class, holding its own independent data even though it shares the class's blueprint and methods with every other instance.

**Integer division** (Chapter 5). Division that discards any remainder, common when both operands are whole numbers in many languages, though some languages, including Python 3 and JavaScript, return a floating-point result instead.

**Interpreter** (Chapter 21). A program that reads and executes source code directly, translating and running each instruction as it goes, rather than compiling the whole program in advance.

**Iteration** (Chapter 7). Repeating a set of instructions, typically using a loop.

**JIT compilation** (Chapter 21). Short for just-in-time compilation: compiling frequently used sections of bytecode into real machine code while a program is actually running, rather than entirely in advance.

**Lambda** (Chapter 18). A function defined without a name, typically written inline exactly where it's needed. Also called an anonymous function.

**Local scope** (Chapter 14). The visibility given to a variable declared inside a function, making it accessible only within that function.

**Loop** (Chapter 7). A construct that repeats a block of instructions, either for as long as a condition holds (while) or a set number of times (for).

**Map** (Chapter 16). A collection that stores values associated with a key rather than a numeric position, also called a dictionary in some languages.

**Memory management** (Chapter 21). The process of deciding when memory is no longer needed and can be reused, handled either manually by the programmer or automatically through garbage collection.

**Method** (Chapter 20). A function that belongs to a class and operates on the data of a specific instance.

**Modulo** (Chapter 5). An operator, usually %, that returns the remainder left over after division.

**Module** (Chapter 23). A self-contained unit of code, generally corresponding to a single file, that can define its own variables, functions, and classes and choose which of them to expose to other files.

**Mutability** (Chapters 4, 8). The ability of a value or collection to be changed after it's created. Arrays are mutable in most languages, at least in their existing contents; strings generally are not.

**Nested collection** (Chapter 16). A collection whose values are themselves collections, such as an array of arrays or a map of maps.

**Null** (Chapter 13). A special value, also called nil in some languages, representing that a reference-type variable doesn't currently point to anything.

**Object** (Chapter 20). A specific instance of a class, bundling data together with the behavior that acts on it.

**Operator** (Chapter 5). A symbol that performs an operation on one or two pieces of data and produces a result, such as +, ==, or &&.

**Output** (Chapter 3). Data a program produces and makes visible, most simply as text printed to a console.

**Parameter** (Chapter 10). A placeholder variable named in a function's own definition, given a real value (the argument) each time the function is called.

**Pointer** (Chapter 17). A variable whose value is a memory address, referring to where a piece of data actually lives rather than holding that data directly.

**Recursion** (Chapter 15). A function that calls itself, using a base case to stop and a recursive case that moves closer to that base case with every call.

**Reference type** (Chapter 13). A type whose variable stores a reference to data held elsewhere in memory, rather than the data itself. Assigning a reference type to a new variable copies the reference, not the underlying data.

**Return value** (Chapter 10). The value a function hands back to whatever called it, using a return statement.

**Runtime error** (Chapter 11). An error that occurs while a program is actually running, as opposed to one caught before execution begins.

**Scope** (Chapter 14). The region of a program in which a particular variable is visible and usable.

**Set** (Chapter 16). A collection that holds only unique values, with no effect from adding a value that's already present.

**Stack** (Chapter 14). A highly organized, fast region of memory used primarily for local variables and for tracking which function called which. Data on the stack disappears automatically when the function that owns it finishes running.

**Stack overflow** (Chapters 14, 15). An error caused by exceeding the available space on the stack, commonly the result of recursion that never reaches its base case.

**Static and dynamic typing** (Chapter 13). In a statically typed language, a variable's type is fixed and checked before the program runs. In a dynamically typed language, type is not checked until the program is actually running.

**String** (Chapters 4, 9). Text, represented as a sequence of characters and usually written as a literal inside quotation marks.

**String interpolation** (Chapter 9). A way of embedding variables directly inside a string without repeatedly breaking out of it with concatenation.

**Strong and weak typing** (Chapter 13). In a strongly typed language, mixing incompatible types in an operation is generally refused. In a weakly typed language, the language often attempts a conversion automatically instead.

**Struct** (Chapter 20). Short for structure: a way of grouping several related pieces of data together under one name, without necessarily bundling in behavior the way a class does.

**Transpiler** (Chapter 21). A tool that translates source code from one high-level language into another high-level language, rather than down into machine code or bytecode.

**Tuple** (Chapter 10). A lightweight, ordered, fixed-size group of values treated as a single unit, often used to return more than one value from a function.

**Two's complement** (Chapter 12). The near-universal method modern computers use to represent negative numbers in binary, chosen because it lets addition and subtraction use the same hardware circuitry regardless of sign.

**Type** (Chapter 4). A classification of what kind of data a variable holds, such as a number, string, or boolean, which determines what operations make sense on it.

**Type conversion** (Chapter 4). Explicitly telling a program to reinterpret a piece of data as a different type, also called casting.

**Value type** (Chapter 13). A type whose variable stores its actual data directly. Assigning a value type to a new variable copies the data itself, leaving the two variables independent.

**Variable** (Chapter 4). A named place to keep a piece of data so a program can refer to it again, use it in calculations, or change it as execution continues.

**Virtual machine** (Chapter 21). A program that runs bytecode, either by interpreting it directly or by compiling frequently used sections of it into real machine code while the program runs.

## Where This Goes Next

This glossary covers vocabulary. For the ideas themselves, worked through one at a time, that's what the book is for. For a chance to actually run some of them, visit gibidda.com/underneath-the-syntax.

# About the Author

Edison Mooers has spent more than three decades writing software, from COBOL to modern enterprise architecture, and currently leads a software engineering team building AI-integrated tools for chemical process research. He is self-taught, having learned to program as a kid on a hand-me-down computer with nothing but a manual, and later completed both a bachelor's and a master's degree in Information Technology while working full-time. He writes, builds, and publishes independently under Gibidda Press, including QF Code, a programming language for beginners built around the same philosophy as this book. Find more of his work at gibidda.com and edisonmooers.com.

# Continue with the Free Companion

*Underneath the Syntax: Try It in QF Code* is a free companion to this book. The main book is deliberately language-neutral; the companion does the opposite on purpose, using guided exercises and runnable examples written in **QF Code™** to put the ideas into practice.

## Why I Created QF Code

New programmers are often asked to learn two things at once: the ideas that make programming work and the syntax rules of a particular language. I created QF Code to separate those problems.

QF Code is a browser-based programming language designed for clarity, consistency, and low cognitive friction. It lets learners focus first on what the code means, while building skills that transfer cleanly to other programming languages.

**Read or download the companion free at: gibidda.com/syntax**

www.ingramcontent.com/pod-product-compliance
Lightning Source LLC
LaVergne TN
LVHW022226200926
848481LV00006B/2141